A Theological Journey

John F. Patrick

ISBN: 978-1-906018-04-7

A CIP catalogue for this book is available from the National Library.

CONTENTS

INTRODUCTION

THIS BOOK TAKES A THEOLOGICAL JOURNEY through a number of topics which may be of interest to some readers in today's busy world.

The Real Mary

Outlined here are some views on how we can look for and find the real Mary in today's world. It looks at how our coloured view of Mary has contributed to the crisis in Mariology and how we can find the real Mary in the Bible. Included also are some extracts from a talk given by Ivan, one of the visionaries at Medugorje.

The Shepherd and the Psalm

The Shepherd and the Psalm (Psalm 23) is a very old story which I received from a nun and which has no known author. It tells of old Fernando D'Alfonso, a Basque shepherd, one of the best in his district and rightly so, for behind him were at least twenty generations of Iberian shepherds. D'Alfonso was more than a shepherd; he was also a patriarch of his guild, the traditions and secrets of which have been handed down from generation to generation. He was full of the legends, the mysterious and the religious fervour of his native hills.

One night under the clear, starry skies, his sheep bedded down beside a sparkling pool of water he suddenly began a dissertation in a jargon of Greek and Basque. When he had finished, he was asked what he had said. In reply he began to quote the 23rd Psalm. There and then he quoted the shepherd's literal interpretation of this beautiful poem.

What Ecological Crisis?

I have attempted to lay out some of the good, the bad, and the ugly in relation to the ecological crisis we face today. I have outlined the history of the church's attitude to ecology and how it has improved greatly in recent years. I have mentioned some of the common problems we face in Ireland. I have discussed some of the strategies that are being adopted for the future and others that need more study and subsequent implementation. I mentioned how creation and nature and the Trinity are interlinked and could be taught in conjunction with sowing crops and measuring environmental changes.

Go Teach All Nations

This statement in Matthew's gospel is a mission statement which is repeated in a different way in the other gospels and in Acts. The message is as clear today in the post-Vatican II era as it was in the early church. In this essay I examine the response to the statement in the early church and outline that difficult period in history for Christians up to AD 311.

I examined the interpretations of the mission statement in documents from Vatican II and subsequent documents from the Holy See up to the present time. Since the bishops are the successors to the apostles, I studied their recent view from the United States Bishop's Conference in 2005. I researched the location and type of activity being carried out by Irish missionaries abroad and included practical examples of their great work in spite of the difficulties including martyrdom. Since any future effort in carrying out this mission statement is dependent on our youth today, I examined a sample of their views on religion and other matters. I also looked at some key points on ways to improve our understanding of youth today, with a view to involving them more in the life of the church in the future

Finally, I have attempted to show how today's church is imitating the early church; giving examples of new activities and movements.

The Way of the Wise in the Book of Proverbs

I have attempted to set out the principal messages that I considered important in this great book from the Old Testament. This covered the history, literary form, structure and the use of personification and the importance of God. I also sought out the proverbs that I thought were relevant to family, neighbours and society in general. There are some limitations in the proverbs. The most obvious limitation is that the wise men of that time did not know about the afterlife. They felt that wisdom and good living would be fully rewarded in this life. However, this has increased my personal admiration for them. The second deficiency is the wise men's proposal that personal success is the key motive for the practice of justice. The New Testament resolved this by offering another reason in the Kingdom of God as established by Jesus Christ. The third deficiency is the treatment of women as second-class citizens. This was the culture of the time.

What message did I get from reading Proverbs for the first time? Since they are the word of God they will always have an important value. They are the words of wisdom collected by an ancient people as a result of their experiences, which were different from my own. We cannot demand from them the insights which came with the teachings of Jesus. The proverbs show the qualities suitable for sensible living, being prudent and just and willing to forgive, being in control of my tongue and able to correct my children. In Israel at that time men would engage in talk at the gates as the women would look after the house and the children. The last poem urges all husbands to praise their wives and to be grateful to them.

Significant points about Islam and why I find them interesting

Having examined a number of references on Islam, I have learned many points which I have found interesting for the following reasons:

- The history of Islam and its relationship to Christianity.
- The different groups within Islam and why some are so opposed to others.
- The daily prayers and place of worship of Islam.
- The importance of the Qur'an and how it can be misinterpreted just as the Bible has been misinterpreted.

- On the role of women there is an urgent need for a survey to clarify the position for the western world. There is also a need for polititians and journalists and scholars to clarify many of the prevailing misconceptions that exist today.
- I also found the muslim view of the afterlife interesting.

I feel that I have learned a great deal more about Islam which will help me to reduce barriers in the future. Some scholars of Islam feel that the Qur'an could be adapted, so that it would be less uncompromising. However the vision of Jesus was focused on love rather than law. This is seen in the Sermon on the Mount, where one is encouraged to love one's enemies.

The Contribution of Philosophy, Psychology and Science to the Phenomenon of Atheism

Here I have attempted to set out the principal points I consider important. These covered the definition and the history of Atheism. I sought out the views of noted philosophers, a psychologist and other commentators on science and other matters.

Many of us have been blessed with an upbringing in an environment that made belief in God much easier than for many others who have suffered more or have been raised in a spiritually impoverished environment or had other difficulties to cope with.

Pope John Paul II was a philosopher and a great believer in the rights of people to choose which faith they choose to believe in with their own consciences. In this way he was able to open dialogue with many faiths that had previously felt they were being preached at. Scripture makes it clear we are not to judge others, however much we are called to correct evil.

To a person of deep faith no explanation of the existence of God is necessary. To a person who will not believe, no explanation is adequate.

Marriage at the Heart of God's Plan

I have set out my reasons for believing that marriage is at the heart of God's Plan. Marriage is seen as a good plan by most societies and religions in the world and the best way to organize itself and its society. I have examined marriage in the Old Testament from the book of Genesis up to the time of Jesus. In the New Testament I looked at the culture of the Romans and how the Church accepted much of that culture on marriage. In the New Testament I have mentioned the teaching of Jesus to the Pharisees as outlined in Mark's Gospel.

I used information from Vatican 11 on marriage and the arguments over marriage being a contract or a covenant which need the involvement of married people to help in producing more understandable wording. I mentioned how God's plan for marriage is being rejected in today's world and some of the consequences. Finally I found two prayers for married couples, one from the Old Testament and the other from today.

What did I get from this article? This topic has made me more aware of marriage as a sacrament and a covenant for life and that the Holy Spirit is always available to help in difficult times.

I

THE REAL MARY

THE REAL MARY

I FEEL COMPELLED TO WRITE THIS ARTICLE for a number of reasons. In today's world transport and communications have improved greatly, however, the number of people who have never heard of Jesus is increasing. I believe that if we lose Mary we will also lose Jesus. It is also my opinion that if we look in the Bible we will find the real Mary and her objectives.

In this article I discuss the image we had of Mary in the past, and how the plastic image does not represent Mary, the first century Palestinian housewife. I also discuss the crisis in Mariology today and how this manifests itself but this article concentrates mainly on finding Mary in the Bible. In conclusion I also provide a extracts from a talk given recently by Ivan, one of the visionaries at Medugorje.

Mary in the Past

Dogmatic presentation of Mary has been emphasised greatly in the past under four dogmas: Mary the Mother of God, from the council of Epheses (AD 431), Mary the Perpetual Virgin, Mary the Immaculate Conception (1854), The Assumption of Mary into Heaven (1954).

Apart from the four dogmas, which form the central core of the Catholic church's belief, there are also two important doctrines associated with Mary as follows: Mary as co-redemptrix i.e. Mary as mother of Christ and also her personal holiness. The other doctrine is Mary as mediatrix from her role as mediator. In addition we need to discover Mary in the Bible

Traditional presentation of Mary made her out to be a privileged person. It led to more admiration than imitation. In this democratic age privileged people tend to be looked on as irrelevant. She is a model in her faith and holiness which needs to be stressed. Traditional presentation may have suited a male dominated church in that she was presented as passively obedient and someone who understood God's will perfectly. The biblical accounts don't reflect this view.

The cultural and political exploitation of Mary started in the 10th century when ruling classes exploited her image. She was more like the maids in the palaces or the peasant woman. This may have been a reaction against the prevailing image of Jesus as a stern judge. This tended to destroy the real Mary. The gospels present Mary as a woman of faith, who put all her trust in God, and her life was a pilgrimage of faith. Mary conceived Jesus first in her heart and then in her womb.

Crisis in Mariology

Today there is a crisis in Mariology which may have begun after Vatican II for a number of reasons. There has been a tendency to give Mary a role of mediator and intercessor beyond human powers. The rise of feminism may also have contributed to the questioning of the traditional presentation of Mary who was sometimes used in the past as a weapon for male chauvinism. Some people believe that Vatican II has contributed to the crisis in Mariology indirectly. Vatican II did not have a special constitution on Mary, but included her as part of the constitution of the church in Chapter 8 of *Lumen Gentium*. There was only a majority of 40 votes against a special constitution out of a total of 2188 votes. At the same time Vatican II was unambiguous in its criticism concerning excesses of exaggeration and sentimentality. It warned against a type of schoolgirl infatuation with an ideal beautiful woman. Protestants often referred to the excesses in the Catholic approach to Marian doctrine and devotion.

How is this crisis manifested?

After Vatican II there were fewer theological books and articles on Mary. There has been a decline in Marian novenas and a big decline in the recitation of the rosary. There has been a widespread failure to appreciate the place of Mary in Christian worship. Sermons on Mary are less frequent than in the past. Many people believe that if we lose Mary we will also lose Jesus. Her main objective today seems to be to lead all people to God.

Finding Mary in the Bible

Mary in the Old Testament.

Obviously there are very few direct references to Mary in the

Old Testament, but it does not mean there are no references whatever. The Old Testament references to Mary are typographical, that is, they serve as a prelude or symbol for an event in the New Testament. Mary is prefigured in the Old Testament several times. We learn in Genesis of the promise of a redeemer from the woman (Genesis 3:15). Eve herself, the mother of all the living, prefigures Mary (Genesis 3:20). The matriarchs in the Old Testament foreshadow Mary and Elizabeth in the New Testament. Ester and Judith, with their sense of survivability and indestructible spiritual strength personify Israel, and in Hosea woman and Israel become interchangeable (Hosea 11:19).

The whole of Israel looks to the fulfilment in the Messiah. Mary the young Jewish virgin, became a symbol for Israel itself, and the one that bore Jesus, the Messiah. In Genesis, Eve has symbolically become the mother of all the living. Mary is the mother of the church. In its turn the church is the mother of all those who are baptized in the body of Christ, which gradually extends to all people. The Collegeville Bible Commentary sums up the passages from Hosea as follows: "If ever there was an Old Testament discourse wrapping God in the warm flesh of human priesthood, this is it." [1]

Isiah 7:14–15 tells us "The virgin is with child and bears a son and calls his name Emmanuel. He will live on curds and honey by the time he learns to refuse evil and choose good." The prophesy about the virgin giving birth is one of the most important in the bible. [2] The prophet was angry with King Ahaz (a descendant of David) who was speaking to Yahweh. These descendants of David, whom God has always protected, are useless. Another descendant of David will be able to bring salvation to God's people. Yahweh is preparing to send him. But before this future king may bring peace, he will be raised humbly. Before that Ahaz and his absurd followers will certainly bring total ruin to the country. Emmanuel means God with us. Why is virgin mentioned? The term meant young girl when it was used. Here Isaiah is referring to the future mother of the King Messiah, and we know that she is the Virgin Mary.

Mary in the New Testament

The Annunciation (Luke 1:26–38)

> God had no need of a woman to make a human body, but He wanted to have a mother for His son, and for Mary to be that mother, it was necessary that God looked upon her with greater love than He had for any other creature. Thus Mary is called 'full of grace.' Grace is what we call the power God has to heal our spirit, to instill in us the disposition to believe, so that the expression of love comes from us in a spontaneous and unexpected way…Mary is really full of grace because Jesus was born of her as He is born of the Father. He is not her son only through the flesh, but He is son of her soul and of her faith, because she is the servant of the Lord. This is why the church believes Mary has a unique role in the work of salvation. [3]

Jesus born of a virgin mother. (Matt 1:18–25)

> The story of Jesus' birth is really an extension of the geneality. The primary concern is Jesus' right to a place in the messianic genealogy through Joseph, and its climax comes in

> Joseph's resolve to make Jesus a Davidic child by assuming the responsibilities of paternity.[4]

As a devout observer of the Old Testament, Joseph felt he could not take Mary as his wife (Deut. 22:23–27). To avoid subjecting Mary to the shameful trial of a woman suspected of adultery he decided to divorce her. This was his prerogative as noted in Deuteronomy 24:1. The dream that Joseph had, allayed his fears. Not only had Mary not been raped or seduced, but this child had been conceived by the Holy Spirit and deserves the name, son of David, Jesus, and Emmanuel, Joseph took Mary as his wife. The statement in verse 25 that he did not have sexual relations with her before the birth of Jesus neither confirms or denies the perpetual virginity of Mary. Mary as perpetual virgin is a dogma of the church:

> We need to distinguish between physical virginity and spiritual virginity (physical virginity ultimately is a symbol of her total engagement with God). Virgin birth is not a statement about Mary, but about Jesus, about His transcendence.[5]

Mary was about to be married and was engaged to Joseph, which according to Jewish law gave them the rights of marriage. Under these conditions her words at the announciation—"I do not know man"—would not make sense if Mary had not decided to remain a virgin. Many people are surprised by such a decision on Mary's part. How could she think about remaining a virgin in marriage, especially among a people who did not value virginity? Many people in non-Catholic churches, when they read in the gospels about the brothers of

Jesus (Mark 3:19), simply conclude that Mary had other children after Jesus.

The Catholic Church never doubted that Mary was a virgin, and that Jesus was her only son as he is the only son of the Father. Why then does it speak of brothers and sisters?

In Hebrew any relation can be called brother or sister. In John 19:25, Mary is mentioned as a sister of Mary the mother of Jesus. This Mary was the mother of James and Joset who are called brothers of Jesus in Mark 6:3. Also in the first Christian community, when the gospels were written, there was a very influential group composed of Jesus' relatives and townmates of Jesus from Nazareth. These were called "brothers of the Lord" and one of them, James, became bishop of the Jerusalem community.[6] If the virginity of Mary was a very unusual commitment, it would not have been unusual for Joseph to choose a life if celibacy like monks. Joseph surely was not going to be an obstacle to Mary but rather a support. [7]

The Visitation (Luke 1: 39–56)

> Luke brings together the two mothers-to-be so that both might praise the God active in their lives and that Elizabeth's child might be presented as a "precursor" of Mary's child. The leaping of Esau and Jacob in Rebecca's womb (Gen 25:22) presents a parallel to the "Leaping" of John. Such activity is a foreshadow of future relationships. The context makes clear that by leaping, John recognises his lord Jesus. Through the power of the Holy Spirit Elizabeth is empowered to interpret the leaping of John.[8]

"And how does this happen to me that the mother of my lord

should come to me," recalls the words of King David when the Ark of the Covenant was being brought back to Jerusalem after being captured by the Phillistines: "How can the ark of the Lord come to me?" (2 Samuel 6:9)

The Magnificat

This prayer shows Mary as a very strong, intelligent and capable woman. The hymn is strongly influenced by the canticle sung by Hannah, the mother of Samuel the prophet, after the birth of her son through divine intervention (1 Samuel 2:1–10).Both canticles see these actions of God as part of a longstanding process of overthrowing proud human expectations and exalting the lowly.

The Nativity (Luke 2:3–7)

As there was a census, the family had to go to King David's town of Bethlehem to be registered as they belonged to the family of David. The swaddling clothes and the manger illustrate the poverty and humility of Jesus' birth, but the wrappings are also a subtle reminder of his royalty. Hidden here is a parallel with the birth of King Solomon: "In swaddling clothes and with constant care I was nurtured. For no king has any different origin of birth" (Wis. 7:4–5). The humble king's birth is proclaimed first to the lowly. It is through these lowly ones that the message of salvation comes to the whole people of Israel (Luke 2:3–7): "They were in Bethlehem when the time came for her to have her child, and she gave birth to a son, her first born. She wrapped him in swaddling clothes and laid him in a manger, because there was no place for them in the living room."

There have been many departures from faith during the past twenty centuries; one of the most common has been to misunderstand how God became human. We say that Mary is the mother of God, and not only the mother of the man Jesus, because the son of God become man cannot be divided. [9] The census provided Luke with a means of getting Mary and Joseph from Nazareth to Bethlehem, the city of David where the promised heir of David was to be born (Mic 5:1).[10]

The Presentation in the Temple (Luke 2:12–40)

> Jesus' parents obeyed imperial law at the time of his birth; now they are portrayed as observant Jews fulfilling the prescriptions of the religious law concerning circumcision and the presentation and redemption of the first born to the Lord…because the first born son "belongs" to the lord who saved them when the Egyptian first born were destroyed at the Passover (Exod. 13:15)…On this occasion she was to offer a lamb and a pigeon or a turtledove, but a poor couple were permitted to bring only two pigeons or a turtledove. The emphasis is less on the purification of Mary than on the presentation of Jesus in the temple, where he will receive a more official recognition as the promised saviour of Israel.[11]

On blessing the parents, Simeon warns that this child will be a sign opposed and that Mary will be pierced with a sword. Here we are given a foreshadow of Jesus' future. Mary and Joseph must have worried when they heard this.

The Finding of Jesus in the Temple (Luke 3: 41–51)

Every year the parents of Jesus went to Jerusalem for the feast of the Passover which was customary. Jesus, who was twelve years old went with them, and "after three days they found him in the temple, sitting among the teachers, listening to them and asking questions. And all the people were amazed at his understanding and his questions." Seated in the shade of the temple galleries the teachers of the law used to teach groups of pilgrims and dialogue with them. Jesus manifested his independence for the first time.

Mary asked him "Why have you done this to us?"

Then he said to them "Why were you looking for me? Do you not know that I must be in my father's house?"

But they did not understand this answer. Jesus could have asked permission or let his parents know where he was. Actually he achieved radical freedom before returning with them. The power of the Holy Spirit was working within him. From then on he would be obedient but he had shown them that he knew who he was, and that he was capable of any sacrifice or breaking any ties to serve his father.

Luke does not mention anymore about the life of Jesus until he is thirty years old. When reading this text, we should reflect on the respect that parents must have for the vocation of their children and the effort they must make to be able to understand them when they begin to be independent. Instead of speaking of the lost child, it would be more appropriate to say that the young Jesus had found himself.[12]

The Marriage Feast of Cana (John 2: 1–11)

What happened in Cana is a sign which reveals the glory of Jesus and leads those who are open in faith to a deeper understanding of the person of Jesus and look forward to

> Jesus' hour, to his death and resurrection when his glory is fully revealed. [13]

The disciples began to know Jesus but Mary, his mother, already understood and believed in him. What Mary wanted was a miracle or something like it in order to free the groom from embarrassment. His spirit recognised the Holy Spirit, speaking through his mother, and granted his first miraculous sign. This was how Jesus manifested his glory to those who were beginning to discover him. Mary had brought grace to John the Baptist (Luke 1:39) and again she intervenes to hasten the beginnings of the gospel. She will not speak again in the gospel, and her last words are, "Do whatever he tells you." Mary has sensed that Jesus will act, even though his answer remains mysterious to her. Mary seems to have faith that he will intervene.

Mary and John at the Cross. (John 19:26–27)

When Jesus saw the mother, and the disciple, he said to the mother, "Woman, this is your son." Then he said to the disciple, "There is your mother." And from that moment the disciple took her to his own home. Mary has neither spouse nor son who can receive her and, for the Jews, a woman who remains alone would be considered cursed. The fourth Gospel may be presenting Mary beneath the cross in a double role:

- As feminine symbol of mother church, caring for, and placed in the care of, Jesus' disciples, who become her children and, consequently, Jesus' brothers and sisters.
- As woman of the victory, emphasizing the feminine con-

tribution to salvation. The negative biblical portrait of Eva has been replaced by that of the life-giving Ave.[14]

Through the last deed of Jesus, the church discovered something about the mystery of the Christian life. The believer is a member of a spiritual family. As a child needs a father and a mother to grow normally so, too, does the believer need Mary and the heavenly father.[15]

The Pentecost (Acts 1: 12–14, 2: 1–4)

The eleven disciples were present in the upper room in Jerusalem. All of them together gave themselves to constant prayer. With them were some women and also Mary, the mother of Jesus, and his brothers. Mary the mother of Jesus played a decisive role during those days when the apostles tried to reflect together on all they had seen and heard from Jesus, in order to clarify the message they had to give to the world.

Mary, only witness of the announciation and of the private life of Jesus, helped them perceive the mystery of his divine personality. [16]

One reason Luke singled out Mary and the brothers of Jesus maybe that they hear and keep God's word. Another is to draw a parallel between Mary's role in Jesus' birth and her presence at the church's birth at Pentecost, when the Spirit came upon her in a new way. It is not certain the "brothers of Jesus" were considered his blood relatives as Mary's perpetual virginity is a church dogma.'[17]

The Book of Revelations (Rev 12:1–6)

The story of the woman and the dragon draws upon a wealth

of symbolism from the myths of the ancient near east, from Jewish and Greek sources.[18] They all reflect an archetypal symbol of the heavenly mother and her divine child, who are attacked by the evil monster from the waters of chaos. The mother and child must be rescued from the forces of evil.[19]

The imagery makes it clear that the child born to the woman is the Messiah. The traditional Catholic interpretation has been that she is Mary, the mother of Jesus, who is the new Eve. Other suggestions are that she is the heavenly Jerusalem, personified by wisdom or the church.

The following are some extracts from the talk of Ivan, one of the visionaries in Medjugorje

June 14th 2006

He was a sixteen year old at the time of the first apparition. He is not a saint and he is not perfect, but trying to be holy. He has a great desire to be holy. He goes on to say that conversion is a work for a lifetime, everyday to avoid sin, to be open to peace, to the Holy Spirit, and to accept the gospels. He asks himself one question every day: Why did Mary choose him, and is he able to fullfill her wishes?

One day he asked her—Why?

She said, "Dear child, I am not always looking for the best ones."

For twenty-five years he has this great gift of seeing Our Lady every day. This is a great responsibility. God is giving him a lot but asks a lot in return. It lasts for five to ten minutes each day, but it takes a few hours to come down to reality after each vision. He is coming from the light of heaven down to earth and it seems to him as if Mary wants to bring the light of heaven to the earth. The most important messages have to do with peace, conversion, prayer, penance, fasting, forgiveness and hope.

Mary's messages are always simple. It started in 1981 when Mary introduced herself as the Queen of Peace. She said "I have come because my son sends me. Peace must be between God and man."

She said that the world is going through a very difficult situation and the world could destroy itself. Her geatest desire is peace and a mother knows best about peace, peace in the family and peace in the church. She wants to help and encourage and console us and she wants what is good for us. For example she said "Dear children, today more than ever before, the world is going through very difficult moments and the greatest cause is that the world is going to a future without God."

Prayer has disappeared, parents have no time, there is no love and there is no faithfulness. Many homes are broken. There are so many young people who live away from their parents and Mary is crying because there are so many abortions.

Mary says, "Children, I am with you and I wish you to pray. Decide for good against sin."

Mary's messages are very simple and repeated like any mother who tells her children to behave, study, work, and pray. A good mother does not get tired of delivering this message.

We are pilgrims and she says if it comes to a choice between attending an apparition or Mass, that I should choose Mass, because Jesus is present there. We should attend daily Mass and venerate the cross and say the rosary and read scripture and the Bible should be visible in every house. Mary says we should pray with the heart and be filled with peace and joy.

It is difficult to concentrate, so I must do my best and persevere.

We should pray three hours each day. Ivan said he met an Austrian woman and she asked him "How come Mary is looking for three hours? It is a long time." So, time passed and the following year he met her again and she said "Is Mary still looking for three hours?" Ivan said, "No, that has changed. Now it is twenty-four hours."

So, we are selfish and we should be continually in this school of prayer, every day, with no days off. Grace is given to those who pray more. For families, time is not the problem, love is the problem, and Mary wants us to waken up and to make us stronger. Ivan says he will recommend all of us to Mary and he said that Mary looks very beautiful with a grey dress, blue eyes and with a crown of stars, and the picture in the hall that we were in is the nearest but not exact, she is prettier. He asked her the question, how is she so beautiful? She answered him, "Because I love."

Finally, Ivan said that he hopes we will respond to the messages and make the world a better place. He asked us to continue to pray in Medjugorje and at home and desire for peace, pray for peace.

Finally, he said: "Do not be afraid."

Summary

I have outlined my views on how we can look for and find the real Mary in today's world. I mentioned how our coloured view of Mary has contributed to the crisis in Mariology. I discussed how we can find the real Mary in the Bible and I also included some extracts from a talk given by Ivan, one of the visionaries at Medugorje

Conclusions

Mary is the ideal believer and the first disciple. The Gospels present Mary as the woman of faith, who put all her trust in

God like Abraham. Mary's life was a pilgrimage of faith.

Mary is an example of how the poor have mediated God in history through compassion and strength, not violence and despair. Mary is more blessed by what she receives rather than by what she does, and this is illustrated in all the Dogmas on Mary. For the greatest task in the history of salvation God chose a teenager, which proves God's predilection for the young. Mary is a model for all mothers who have lost a son or who have difficulty understanding a son. She accepted her suffering and so made it redemptive. Mary can be seen as the feminine face of God as a way of counteracting the comparative neglect she has suffered. Mary is the mother of the church and we are her sons and daughters. Finally Mary embodies the total self-giving of Jesus for the benefit of others.

Bibliography

Brown, Raymond, Joseph Fitzmyer and Roland Murphy. *The New Jerome Biblical Commentary*. New Jersey: Prentice Hall, 1999.

Christian Community Bible, Catholic Pastoral Edition. Manila: Divine Word Publications, 1991.

Dunne, Rev. T. *Lecture notes (the marriage feast of Cana).* 20/10/05

Kerris, Robert. *The Collegeville Bible Commentary.* Minnesota: Liturgical Press, 1992,

Putti, Joseph. *Lecture notes.* May 2006.

Endnotes

1. Robert Kerris, *The Collegeville Bible Commentary* (Minnesota: Liturgical Press 1992), 505.

2. *Christian Community Bible*, Catholic Pastoral Edition (Manila: Divine Word Publications, 1991), 522.

3. *Christian Community Bible*, Catholic Pastoral Edition (Manila: Divine Word Publications, 1991), 118–119.

4. Robert Kerris, *The Collegeville Bible Commentary* (Minnesota: Liturgical Press 1992), 864.

5. Joseph Putti, *Lecture notes*, May 2006.

6. *Christian Community Bible*, Catholic Pastoral Edition (Manila: Divine Word Publications, 1991), 76.

7. *Christian Community Bible*, Catholic Pastoral Edition (Manila: Divine Word Publications, 1991), 8.

8. Raymond Brown et al, *The New Jerome Biblical Commentary*. (New Jersey: Prentice Hall, 1999), 681.

9. *Christian Community Bible*, Catholic Pastoral Edition (Manila: Divine Word Publications, 1991), 120.

10. Raymond Brown et al, *The New Jerome Biblical Commentary*. (New Jersey: Prentice Hall, 1999), 683.

11. Robert Kerris, *The Collegeville Bible Commentary* (Minnesota: Liturgical Press 1992), 864.

12. *Christian Community Bible*, Catholic Pastoral Edition (Manila: Divine Word Publications, 1991), 122.

13. Rev. T. Dunne, *Lecture notes (The Marriage Feast of Cana)*, September 2005.

14. Robert Kerris, *The Collegeville Bible Commentary* (Minnesota: Liturgical Press 1992), 1013.

15. *Christian Community Bible*, Catholic Pastoral Edition (Manila: Divine Word Publications, 1991), 225.

16. *Ibid*, 232.

17. Robert Kerris, *The Collegeville Bible Commentary* (Minnesota: Liturgical Press 1992), 1038.

18. *Ibid*, 1284.

18. *Ibid*, 1285.

II

THE SHEPHERD AND THE PSALM

THE SHEPHERD AND THE PSALM

PSALM 23

OLD FERNANDO D'ALFONSO WAS A BASQUE shepherd, one of the best in his district and rightly so, for behind him were at least twenty generations of Iberian shepherds. But D'Alfonso was more that a shepherd; he was a patriarch of his guild, the traditions and secrets of which have been handed down from generation to generation. He was full of the legends, the mysterious and the religious fervour of his native hills.

I sat with him one night under the clear, starry skies, his sheep bedded down beside a sparkling pool of water. As we were preparing to curl up in our blankets he suddenly began a dissertation in a jargon of Greek and Basque. When he had finished, I asked him what he had said. In reply he began to quote the 23rd Psalm. There and then I learned the shepherd's literal interpretation of this beautiful poem.

"David and his ancestors," said D'Alfonso, "know sheep, and their ways, and David has translated a sheep's musing into simple words. The daily repetition of this psalm fills the shepherd with reverence for his calling. Our guild takes this poem as a lodestone to guide us. It is our bulwark when the days are hot or stormy, when the nights are dark, when wild animals surround our bands. Many are the duties of a Holy Land shepherd, whether he lives today or followed the same calling 3000 years ago. Phrase by phrase, it has a well understood meaning for us."

THE LORD IS MY SHEPHERD.

I SHALL NOT WANT.

"Sheep instinctively know," said D'Alfonso, "that before they have been folded for the night, the shepherd has planned out their grazing ground. They do not worry. His guidance has been good in the past, and they have faith in the future because they know he has their wellbeing in view."

HE MAKES ME LIE DOWN IN GREEN PASTURES.

"Sheep graze from about 3.30 in the morning until about 10AM. They then lie down for three or four hours and rest," said D'Alfonso. "When they are contentedly chewing the cud, the shepherd knows they are putting on fat. Consequently the good shepherd starts his flocks out in the early hours on the rougher herbage, moving on through the morning to the richer, sweeter grasses, and coming to a shady place for the forenoon rest in fine green pastures, best grazing of the day. Sheep resting on such happy surroundings feel contentment."

HE LEADS ME BESIDE STILL WATERS

"Every shepherd knows," said the Basque, "that sheep will not drink gurgling water. There are many small springs high in the hills of the Holy Land, whose waters run down the valleys only to evaporate in the desert sun. Although the sheep need the water, they will not drink from these fast-flowing streams. The shepherd must find a place where rocks or erosion have made a little pool, or else he fashions with his hands a pocket sufficient to hold at least a bucketful.

HE RESTORES MY SOUL: HE LEADS ME THROUGH THE PATHS OF RIGHTEOUSNESS: FOR HIS NAME'S SAKE

"In the Holy Land," went on D'Alfonso, "each sheep takes his place in the grazing line in the morning, and keeps the same position throughout the day. Once during the day, however, each sheep leaves its place and goes to the shepherd, whereupon the shepherd stretches out his hand and rubs the animal's nose and ears, scratches its chin, whispers affectionately into its ears.

The sheep meanwhile rubs against his leg, or if the shepherd is sitting down, nibbles at his ear and rubs its cheek against his face. After a few minutes of this communion with the master, the sheep returns to its place in the feeding line."

ALTHOUGH I WALK THROUGH THE VALLEY OF THE SHADOW OF DEATH, I WILL FEAR NO EVIL: FOR YOU ARE BESIDE ME: YOUR ROD AND YOUR STAFF ARE THERE TO COMFORT ME.

"There is an actual valley of the Shadow of Death in Palestine, and every shepherd, from Spain to Dalmatia knows of it. It is south of the Jericho road leading from Jerusalem to the Dead Sea, and it is a narrow defile through a mountain range. Climatic and grazing conditions make it necessary for the sheep to be moved through this valley for seasonal feeding each year.

The valley is 4.5 miles long. Its sidewalls are 1,500 feet high in places, and it is only 10 to 12 ft wide at the bottom. Travel through the valley is dangerous, because its floor has gullies 7 to 8 feet deep. Actual footing on solid rock is so narrow in places that a sheep cannot turn around and it is an unwritten law of shepherds that flocks must go up the valley in the morning hours and down towards the evening, lest flocks meet in the defile. About half-way through the valley the walk crosses from one side to the other at a place where the path is cut in two by a 6 foot gully.

One side of the gully is about 1.5 feet higher than the other; so the sheep must jump across it. The shepherd stands in this break and coaxes or forces the sheep to make the leap. If a sheep slips and lands in the gully, the shepherd's rod is brought into play. The old style crook circles a large sheep's neck or a small sheep's chest, and the animal is lifted to safety. If a modern narrow crook is used, the sheep is caught about the legs and lifted up to the walk. Many wild dogs lurk in the shadows of the valley, looking for prey. The shepherd skilled in using his staff uses it as a weapon. Thus the sheep have learned to fear no evil, even in the Valley of the Shadow of Death, for the master is there to protect them from harm.

YOU PREPARE A TABLE BEFORE ME IN THE PRESENCE OF MY FOES.

"David's meaning is a simple one," said D'Alfonso, "when conditions on the Holy Land sheep pastures are known. Poisonous plants which are fatal to grazing animals abound. Each spring the shepherd must be constantly alert. When he finds the plants, he takes his mattock and goes ahead of the flock, grubbing every stock and root he can see. As he digs out the stocks, he lays them upon little stone pyres, some of which were built by shepherds in Old Testament days and by the morrow they are dry enough to burn. When the pasture is free from poisonous plants, the sheep are led into it and in the presence of their plant enemies, they are free to eat in peace."

YOU ANOINT MY HEAD WITH OIL: MY CUP IS OVERFLOWING

"The sheep flock is led to a gate. The shepherd lays his rod across the top of the gateway just above the backs of the sheep. As each sheep passes, he quickly examines it for briars in the ears, thorns in the cheek or weeping of the eyes from dust or scratches. When such conditions are found, he drops the rod across the sheep's back and it steps out of line. Each sheep's wound is carefully cleansed. Then the shepherd dips his hand into the olive oil and anoints the injury. A large cup is dipped into the jar of water, kept cool by evaporation in the unglazed pottery, and is brought out never full but always overflowing. The sheep will sink its nose into the water right up to the eyes, if fevered, and drink until fully refreshed. When all the sheep are at rest, the shepherd places his staff within reach in case it is needed during the night. Then he wraps himself in his woollen robe and lies down across the gateway, facing the sheep for his night's repose.

"So," concluded D'Alfonso, "after all the care and protection the shepherd has given it, a sheep may well soliloquize in the twilight, as translated into words by David :

SURELY GOODNESS AND MERCY SHALL FOLLOW ME ALL THE DAYS OF MY LIFE: AND I WILL DWELL IN THE HOUSE OF THE LORD AS LONG AS I LIVE.

III

WHAT ECOLOGICAL CRISIS?

WHAT ECOLOGICAL CRISIS?

THE ENGLISH WORD ECOLOGY is taken from the Greek *Oikos* meaning "house, the immediate environment of man." In 1870, the German zoologist Ernst Haechel first gave the word its broader meaning: the study of the natural environment and the relations of organisms to each other and to their surroundings. Since that time, ecology has undergone immense growth and diversification.[1] I decided to write this essay for the following reasons:

My interest in the subject has gradually changed over the years from being involved in production agriculture—maximising profits from production—to maximising profits in an environmentally friendly way—Reps planning.

- Ecology is a major issue for all of us in today's world and tomorrow's world.

- Damaging the environment seems to be the new sin of the 21st century.
- My understanding of God will impact on my attitude to the environment and Ecology.

I was also influenced by the following statement, "Most of today's decision makers will be dead before the planet suffers the full consequences of acid rain, global warming, ozone depletion, widespread desertification, and species loss. Most of today's young voters will be alive."[2]

In this essay I will begin by examining the history of the church and Ecology. I will then look at the challenges and concerns on the environment in Ireland today and a strategy for the future. Finally I will summarise and attempt to draw some conclusions

The History of the Church and Ecology

Creation in the Genesis Priestly account

God created the world because He loved us. He made man the summit of all creation. God reflected on His work and found it good. This is not a scientific explanation of how the world was formed, but a text written to answer the question of how the world was created and why. If God withdrew from the world it would return to chaos. The words used for man to subdue or conquer or have dominion over the world, in hindsight may not have been the best words. Humans as stewards of creation would seem better.

Creation in the Genesis Yahweh account.

This is older than the priestly account and is more earthly. Man was created from the earth. God breathed into him and he shares something of God. God creates a garden and puts mankind into it. Man is given the task to cultivate and keep the garden. The garden is a symbol of God's generosity to the first humans. Man was to work the garden of Eden and care for it (Gen 2:15). He was to use but not abuse it. In today's language his use was to be sustainable.

The covenant with Noah

Noah was instructed to preserve one pair of each species, regardless of its utility to man (Gen 6:19–21) In today's language, biodiversity is good. God makes a covenant not just with Noah, but with all life on earth (Gen: 9:8–17).God promises never again to flood the earth, never again to destroy the habitat of all living creatures. If this is so, our destruction of the environment today works directly against the intent of the covenant. The rainbow should remind us of this, "There is every reason for a Christian today to embrace both the theological teachings of Genesis and the theory of evolution." [3]

The covenant with Israel

The land of Israel is promised to Abraham and his offspring to inherit (Gen 13:14–15) and to be periodically given a chance to recover (Lev.25:3–4). Put these two scriptures together, and it is clear that the land use was to be sustainable. In (Lev.25:23–24) the land is God's and so we can't do as we please with it. In the Old Testament there is constant gratitude to God for what He has given e.g. (Ex. 22:29–31). The Psalms also resort to nature to give praise to God e.g. (Ps.19:65).

The New Testament and the saints

Jesus shows great respect for nature. He has no attachment to wealth or possessions. The parables include seeds, lilies of the field, and birds of the air (Luke 12:27, Matt.6: 26). He told the disciples to preach to all creation. (Mark 16:15).

There were many great saints with a special interest in the environment e.g. Augustine, St.Francis— patron of the environment—and St.Thomas Aquinas. In the Old Irish Church we find St.Bridget who is patron saint of farming and St. Columbian.

Recent Times

Christianity unknowingly contributed to the problem of the environment. The emphasis was on "the other world." The emphasis was on the dignity of the person. The environment did not have a value of its own. Today the emphasis on the environment is related to the goodness of the person. The Protestant churches in recent times were more alert to the environment than the Catholic Church. The World Council of Churches in Vancouver 1983 on *Justice, Peace and the integrity of creation* was a major focus for Christianity. Vatican II did mention the environment in *Gaudium et Spes.* 9 and 34.

Pope John Paul II made a major contribution in *Peace with God the creator* on New Year's Day, 1990 and also in the Catechism of the Catholic Church in 1994. P.516 was helpful.

These were followed by *Evangelium Vitae* in 1995 and also in 2001 *God made man steward of creation.*

The summit on sustainable development in 2002 is a more

recent document. The contributions of individuals like Fr. Sean McDonagh have been extremely valuable.

The Challenges and Concerns on the environment in Ireland today

The following are some of the major environmental challenges in Ireland today: Water quality, air quality and global warming, disposal of waste, and the number and type of habitats.

Water quality

In the EPA survey (2000 to 2003) the quality of water improved slightly from the previous survey (1998 to 2000). Approx 30% of our water needs some improvement. The quality is in the top category in the EU. The next question is who are the main contributors to the problem. Industry, urban and other sources contribute 50% of the problem. Agriculture contributes 50%. This figure will be reduced in the coming years due to reduced fertiliser, increased storage of slurry and probably less livestock. The Nitrogen Directive being negotiated at present will affect dairy farmers and pig farmers and some others in that they will have to reduce their stock or rent more land. Industry and urban areas will also have to make a bigger effort in the future.

Air Quality

Carbon emissions in Ireland have risen 23% from 1990 to 2006. We are allowed a 13% increase up to 2012. Emissions from cars, lorries buses, planes, industry, agriculture and housing are the main cause of the problem.

The breakdown is as follows in 2006:

- Transport 17%
- Agriculture 29%
- Industry 10%
- Home heating 10%
- Energy production 25%

Per Capita Ireland is the highest in the EU. All of these gases lead to global warming. Extra forestry can use up some of this and help to reduce our fines under the Kyoto agreement. Many other gases, aerosols etc., release chemicals that are damaging to the Ozone layer with subsequent health risks.

Industrial and domestic waste

This is a major problem in Ireland at present with most of the waste going to landfill, some of which are illegal. In some cases it is being transported from one county to another e.g. Clare to Tipperary and in other cases some of it is exported e.g. to Dublin. The targets outlined by local authorities on waste management are broadly, 40% Recycling, 40% Thermal treatment and 20% to landfill. I feel that there will be a lot of agitation and political manoeuvrings before this target is reached.

Habitats

Forestry at 10% of the land in Ireland is considered too low in relation to other countries. The proportion of hardwood to conifer at a minimum of 10% on new planting is considered too low. Single species forestry could not be considered as a habitat.

In 2002 less than 20% of our bogs had a conservation value. The good ones contain many rare species of butterfly, dragonfly, snails, birds and plant life. In 2002 the EU said that Ireland declared an insufficient number of habitats under the list of habitats in the directive. As a consequence proceedings were taken against Ireland in 2004. In his article on biodiversity and the Celtic tiger, Richard Nairn reviewed the Irish government's record on protecting biodiversity. The Reps scheme was viewed as a success with many farmers farming in an environmentally friendly manner. He pointed out that there is insufficient support for intensive farmers to change to organic farming. He also mentioned that there is little implementation of the law on protecting rare species of plants.[4]

A Strategy for the future

The Church

The attitude of the Christian churches on the environment is critical to sustaining a continuous effort for improvement. This is a great opportunity to involve young people in religion as they can understand how God and the environment are so closely related. Very often they cannot understand the terminology used by the state. Unfortunately, the Christian churches have been slow to recognise the attack on life which is so relentless today. [5] Fr.McDonagh in *Death of life* goes on to state that Catholic universities and colleges ought to be at the forefront in tracking endangered species and supporting a variety of remedial strategies. He also suggests that local churches should set aside one day each year to celebrate the gift of all life on earth. My own personal opinion is that this idea could be associated with a harvest festival which could be interdenominational with an appropriate and agreed service. This is, after all, God's creation. Only if we know it will we be able to celebrate and promote this love of life in the face of the culture of violence and death which is so prevalent in our times. Protecting life ought surely to be the vocation of every Christian today.[6]

Government

In an article in the Irish Independent newspaper of Dec. 23rd 2006, it was claimed that the minimum net cost of meeting our requirements under the Kyoto agreement for the period 2008 to 2012 would be €675 million at €15 per tonne. At the EU reserve price of €100 per tonne on future carbon trades the cost would be over €2 billion. It is expected that the taxpayer will pay most of this. Ireland only produces 15% of its energy requirements .The rest is imported.

If we continue our present policy the majority of our energy requirements will come from a gas pipeline which goes all the way to Russia and we should remember that we are at the wrong end of it. There is an urgent need to increase the amount of energy we produce to 50% over the next fifteen years. On the positive side the number of farmers in the Reps scheme has increased to 50,000. Also the recent WEE directive of 2004 is in operation and forcing the Government to manage the 50,000 tonnes of electronic waste we generate each year.

Schools

Getting students in schools to plant native trees in their schools and to take responsibility for maintaining the labels is important. In the national school I attended two students were obliged to measure the rainfall each day and record it. The story of creation is much more meaningful for a young person if it is taught in conjunction with nature and the Trinity.

Genetically modified foods

The present EU policy on genetically modified foods, while unsatisfactory to many people, does offer some protection in that it will only recommend a few varieties each year that have been fully tested. This is much better than a broad approval which would be extremely dangerous.

Evangelium Vitae, 1995

> The dominion granted to man by the creator is not an absolute power, or can we speak of a freedom to "use and abuse" or to dispose of things as one pleases. The limitation imposed from the beginning by the creator himself and expressed symbolically by the prohibition not to "eat fruit of the tree" (Gen 2: 16–17) shows clearly enough that, when it comes to the natural world, we are subject not only to biological laws but also to moral ones, which cannot be violated with impunity.[7]

Summary

In this essay I have attempted to lay out some of the good, the bad, and the ugly in relation the ecological crisis we face today. I have outlined the history of the church's attitude to ecology and how it has improved greatly in recent years. I have mentioned some of the common problems we face in Ireland. I have discussed some of the strategies that are being adopted for the future and others that need more study and subsequent implementation. I mentioned how creation and nature and the trinity are interlinked and could be taught in conjunction with planting and measuring environmental changes.

Conclusions

I feel that this essay has helped to improve and renew my limited knowledge of ecology and my awareness of the crisis we face. As an example of this, my view of a hedgerow has progressed from being an obstruction to production in the 1960s and 1970s to being a nature corridor for wildlife which expresses itself in all its diversity which can bring glory to both God and man if cared for in an environmentally friendly way.

The future of our church and the environment are closely linked together. There is an urgent need for courses in the "theology of ecology." There is a great deal of knowledge in government offices that is not being released in a manner that is attractive and understandable to the public. There is nothing we have more in common than the air we breathe, the water we drink, and the climate we and all God's creatures live in. Because these things cross the boundaries between nations, our response must be local, national, and also global. [8]

Bibliography

Ricklets, Robert. New York: W.H.Freeman & Co., 1990.

World Commission on Environment and development, Oxford: Oxford University Press, 1987.

Edwards, Fr. Denis, *The God of Evolution*, New York: Paulist Press, 1999.

Nairn, Richard, *Bio-diversity and the Celtic Tiger*, Wild Ireland Nov–Dec. 2002.

McDonagh, Fr. Sean SSC, *The Death of Life*, Dublin: Columba Press, 2004.

Pope John Paul II, *Evangelium Vitae* 29, 1995.

http://www.alanmarshall.org/essay/christians&environment.htm

Endnotes

1. Robert Ricklets, (New York: W.H. Freeman & Co., 2005), Cover page.
2. *World Commission on Environment and Development*, (Oxford: Oxford University Press, 1987), 1.
3. Fr. Denis Edwards, *The God of Evolution*, (New York: Paulist Press 1999), 13.
4. Richard Naim, Biodiversity and the Celtic Tiger, (Article in Wild Ireland, Nov–Dec, 2002) 25–27.
5. Fr. Sean McDonagh SSC, *The Death of Life*, (Dublin: Columba Press, 2004), 149.
6. Ibid. 151.
7. Pope John Paul II, *Evangelium Vitae* 29, 1995.
8. http://www.alanmarshall.org/essay/christians&environment.htm

IV

GO TEACH ALL NATIONS

GO TEACH ALL NATIONS

I have a number of reasons for choosing this title. Firstly, I am very impressed with the statement in Matthew 28:16–20, "Therefore go and make disciples of all nations, baptizing them in the name of the Father and of the Son and of the Holy Spirit, and teach them to fulfil all that I have commanded you. I am with you always until the end of the world." The New Jerome Bible Commentary states "This brief ending is so rich that it would be hard to say more or greater things in the same number of words." [1]

This title also enables me to involve the three subject areas of Scripture, Church History and Spirituality and, further, I feel that this is a critical time for the missionary spirit, and so I feel that this subject is worthy of detailed study.

Rather than examine this topic over a long period of history I have selected two periods: The Early church and the post-Vatican period.

Chapter 1—The meaning and source of Go Teach All Nations—will deal with the meaning of this statement at the time it was made. I will also examine similar statements that occur in the gospels according to Mark, Luke and John and the Acts of the Apostles.

Chapter 2—The response in the early church—will deal with the response to this statement in the early church up to the time of Constantine. This will include a brief history of the period up to AD 311. Since the Acts of the Apostles is a basic book of the early church, I will examine this book in great detail. The influence of St. Paul in missionary work is of great importance since he is more responsible than any other for the spread of Christianity.

In chapter 3—The response in Vatican II and subsequent documents—I will study and summarize the most up-to-date documents from the Holy See in this period including *Ad Gentes*, *Redemptoris Missio*, and statements from Bishops' conferences.

In chapter 4—Reponse in today's Ministry— I will look at examples of the responses of missionary priests, and the religious in three continents. I will also look at youth as a source of a response in the future. I will show some progress that has been made in trying to imitate the early church.

Finally, I will write about my vision of the challenges and opportunities that lie ahead for the future.

THE MEANING AND SOURCE OF GO TEACH ALL NATIONS

In Matthew's Gospel (Matt 28:16–20)

This was Jesus' last instruction to his disciples before the ascension:

> As for the eleven disciples, they went to Galilee, to the mountain where Jesus had told them to go. When they saw Jesus they bowed before him although some doubted. Then Jesus approached them and said, 'I have been given all authority in heaven and on earth. Therefore go and make disciples from all nations. Baptise them in the name of the Father and of the son and of the Holy Spirit and teach them to fulfil all I have commanded you. I am with you always until the end of this world.

Jesus sent his disciples to evangelise the world—to make

disciples of all nations. He was following the example of Jewish teachers of his time. Jesus gathered around him a group of disciples who lived with him. They knew each other by sharing everyday life. The same is true today. Evangelisation implies interpersonal sharing. To evangelise means to help someone ponder on their former experiences until they can recognise in the person of Christ, in his death and resurrection that path that lights up their own life. That was what Jesus did for his apostles, showing them that the whole Bible, all past experiences of their race, foretold his death and resurrection. [2]

Note: Regarding the word "Teach": *The original translation from Greek in the Synoptic Gospels was "Teach" but some translations changed this to "Make disciples from..." including the bible I am using.*

This is the same message the Catholic church of today reveals to people. Those who believe will be baptised in the name of the Father and the son and the Holy Spirit, the three persons Christ taught us about. He named them separately because the Father is not the son and the son is not the Holy Spirit. In spite of that they are the same God:

> On entering the church the baptised will enter into communion with the Father, with the son and with the Holy Spirit. The Church is before anything else, communion. [3]

I am with you always

The first Christians thought that Christ would come back soon, but by the time the Gospels were written, they understood that history had not reached its end. Jesus had committed himself fully to the Church, just as God had committed himself to the children of Israel.

The Gospel of Matthew was written for the Christian communities in which the majority were Jews. Therefore, it emphasises that Jesus was the Messiah expected by the Jews, and uses many quotations from the Old Testament which foretold the Messiah and described His ways (Matt 4:14; 8:17 and 12:17). Matthew's Gospel repeats this many times. Jesus knew they would reject His message of the kingdom of God and so the Church should address the pagan nations:

> For Matthew, Jesus is first the teacher of humankind. His teaching and parables show us a way to perfection and lay down the guidelines for community, sharing in a church of the poor where everyone is equal. [4]

The New Jerome Biblical Commentary has wonderful things to say about this statement, "This brief ending is so rich that it would be hard to say more or greater things in the same number of words." [5] The worship of the eleven apostles shows their faith even though mixed with doubt. This experience, which is human, gives hope to us today. There are three parts to the farewell words of Jesus, as they refer to the past, the present and the future. All authority has been given in the past i.e. the authority of the kingdom of God.

The missionary commission concerns the present. It contains a general command to go forth and make disciples and their two subordinate clauses, which explains how this is to be done.

All nations

This universal call applies to all peoples including their cultures, and even Jewish people who are not yet disciples.[6] This command comes as somewhat of a surprise, but had been hinted at previously.

Father, Son, Spirit

> This triadic formula may have its Old Testament roots in the apocalyptic triad of God, son of man or elect one and Angel found in Dan 7, Ezek1, Enoch 14. Circumcision is not mentioned probably because of Acts 15:1–29. Teaching them to observe all that I have commanded you. The disciples are to carry on Jesus' teaching ministry, thus laying the foundation for Christian education, theology and other intellectual work. The subject matter of these teachings is the great discourses of Matthews Gospel, but especially, the Sermon on the Mount, which interprets the Old Testament. [7]

The future support "I am with you"—meaning I am and will continue to be—means the divine presence will be with His people as they make decisions, study, pray, preach, baptise and teach.

The Collegeville Bible commentary indicates that the doubts of the apostles vanish quickly:

> The disciples are to share their discipleship with all people (not simply their fellow Jews) and to hand on Jesus' teaching to them. The largely Jewish community for which Matthew wrote his Gospel probably needed some encouragement to share their faith with non-Jews, and the statement in verse

19 was most likely understood as a reference to the Gentile mission. [8]

The promise assures us that the spirit of the risen Jesus will guide and protect the Church during this time: "Matthew brings the story begun by Mark to its logical conclusion: Jesus' appearance in Galilee and commission to the disciples to proclaim the good news about them." [9]

In Mark's Gospel (Mark 16:14–16)

After Jesus showed himself to the eleven while they were at table. He reproached them for their unbelief and stubbornness in refusing to believe those who had seen him after He had been raised. Then He told them "Go out to the whole world and proclaim the good news to all creation. He who believes and is baptised will be saved, he who refuses to believe will be condemned"

In verse 8 there is an abrupt ending of Mark's Gospel. We were looking forward to the meeting between Jesus and the disciples in Galilee, but it does not take place why? We do not know: We find only a series of brief references to Jesus appearances after his resurrection.

"Proclaim the good news to all creation." The good news is the seed that will be planted in the world and will flourish in proper time, in every field of human activity. Salvation is not a matter of saving isolated souls or individual beings. The Gospel is to be proclaimed to all creation in all activities and acts of those who have been renewed by Baptism. They are to be the yeast that transforms human history.' [10]

Mark, who was with Peter and Paul in Rome, put together his Gospel from these accounts adding many details about Jesus he had received from Peter. The so called shorter ending when read immediately after 16:8 was another attempt by the early church to end Mark's Gospel more smoothly. It is probably more acceptable to women. Although the church has recognised this "added ending" as worthy of inclusion in the inspired text, none of them is as inspiring and involving as Mark's own. Mark's abrupt ending leaves it up to his readers to "complete" his Gospel in their lives. [11]

Mark's Gospel was probably written for Greek speaking non Jewish Christians in Rome, approximately AD 60–70. It is generally accepted that his was the first Gospel written and that portions of the other synoptic Gospels used Mark as a source. According to Acts, a group of Christians regularly met in the house of Mark's mother in Jerusalem, and John Mark himself is named as the companion of Paul and Barnabus in their early missionary work (Acts 12:25, 15:37–41).

Although Mark left them, Paul mentions him favourably in two of his later letters (Colossians 4:10, Philemon 24). He is also spoken of with affection in 1 Peter 5:13, and this may be evidence for associating him with Peter as well as with Paul.

In Luke's Gospel (Luke 24:44–49)

> Then Jesus said to them, "Remember the words I spoke to you when I was still with you. Everything written about me in the Law of Moses, the prophets and the Psalms had to be fulfilled." Then he opened their minds to understand the Scriptures and He went on, "You see what was written; the Messiah had to suffer and on the third day rise from the

> dead. Then repentance and forgiveness in His name would be proclaimed to all the nations, beginning from Jerusalem. Now you shall be witnesses to this. And this is why I will send you what my father promised. So remain in the city until you are invested with power from above."

The preaching to all nations also means education of the nations and even of international society. This is something, which takes longer than ten or a hundred years. By saying "You shall be witnesses to these things" Jesus is calling his apostles to be the official witnesses of his gospel and to be the ones who will judge authentic faith.

Luke's cultural background was Greek and he was writing for Greek people. He omitted several details from Mark dealing with Jewish laws and customs, which would seem hard for his readers to understand. Luke dedicates his work to Theophilus who may have been a well-to-do Christian. Luke probably gave him his manuscript with the expectation that several copies would be made at his expense.

Luke makes it clear that those who follow Jesus do not first need to become Jews in order to be Christians. Jesus had come to be a light to the gentiles also. Luke 2:32 "Here is the light you will reveal to all nations." The apostles are excited and tense when Jesus appears to them:

> The Old Testament is referred to in a traditional way by naming its three collections: Law, Prophets and Psalms (usually writings). His words commissioning them as witnesses of His resurrection foreshadow the Acts of the Apostles The "promise" of the Father is the Holy Spirit who will be given

to them to fulfil their mission (Acts 1:8). [12]

How is it possible for Jesus Messiah to preach to all nations in fulfilment of Scriptures? He will do it through Paul and the Church. Thus, Luke achieves his Christological universalism. "Jesus is Messiah in a real and total sense only if God's salvation goes to the ends of the earth through him." [13]

In John's Gospel (John 20:21–23)

> Again Jesus said to them, "Peace be with you. As the Father has sent me, so I am sending you." After saying this he breathed on them and said to them, "Receive the Holy Spirit; for those whose sins you forgive, they are forgiven; for those whose sins you retain they are retained."

Simultaneously, he sends out these disciples just as the Father had sent him (v21). His mission becomes theirs; his work is placed in their hands. And that mission, that work is to manifest God who is love in their words and deeds.[14]

John 13:34–35

> Now I give you a new commandment; Love one another, just as I loved you, you also must love one another. By this everyone will know that you are my disciples if you have love for one another.

John 15:16–17

> You did not choose me; it is I who chose you and sent you to go and bear much fruit. Fruit that will last. And everything you ask the Father in my name, He will give you. So I tell

> you to love one another.

The commandment fits awkwardly into this position since what follows deals with the theme of Jesus' departure. The commandment returns in 15:12–17 and is identified as the criterion of salvation and of knowledge of God. This formulation of the commandment is the distinctive mark of Christian community among outsiders and differs in verse 35 from its use in 1 John to castigate those who create internal division within the community: [15]

> As He leaves, he leaves behind His one essential commandment "love one another" (v.34). It is a new commandment because this mutual love must be modelled on something new—on the love that Jesus shows for his disciples. Mutual love must be the sign, the indispensable sign, of their discipleship.[16]

Time and again, Jesus points out the unique importance of Christian Love. Later, His apostles (John 4:7) and the church would sum up His teaching on Love: Love of God is shown through Love of our neighbour, Love of our neighbour depends on Love of God. What is it to Love God? Christian Love lies not in sentiment or feelings but to do what God wishes at each moment of our lives. What God wishes for us regarding our neighbour is that we render loving service and forgiveness:

> It is now recognised that the background of much of John's Gospel is Jewish and not exclusively Greek…Not only is

there an emphasis throughout the Gospel on the fulfilment of the Old Testament, but the evangelist states his purpose in a very Jewish form. [17]

In The Acts of the Apostles (Acts 1:6–8)

> When they had come together, they asked him "Is it now that you will restore the Kingdom of Israel?" And He answered, "It is not for you to know the time or the moment which the Father has fixed by His own authority. But you will receive power when the holy Spirit comes upon you; and you will be my witnesses in Jerusalem, throughout Judea and Samaria, even to the ends of the earth."

The apostles still identify the reign of God with the liberation of the holy nation, Israel. In fact God's purpose is much wider. The Gospel is to change human history, individuals, cultures, the whole of human reality, only the Father knows the time and the goals of this history about which people today are more and more concerned. [18]

Jesus is no longer visible among us and this is to our advantage, for we must assume our responsibilities. But the Christian community will discover at first with surprise and then with joy that the Spirit of God, Spirit of Jesus is acting in their midst.[19]

Verse 1:8 provides a "table of contents" for Acts. The witness "in Jerusalem" is Acts 2 to 7. "Throughout Judea and Samaria," is from chapters 8 to 12, and "to the ends of the earth" is an echo of Isa 49:6. Both Acts and the Psalms of Solomon, a slightly earlier Jewish writing, apply the phrase "the ends of the earth" to Rome. Acts ends in Rome.[20]

The purpose of Acts

> Though he does not address the public directly, Luke must have hoped that his first readers would learn something from his story to help their own Christian thinking.[21]

John Drane goes on to describe at least 3 primary aims:

- The conviction that Christianity is a faith with potential to change the whole world
- Luke emphasises the fact that Christianity could enjoy a good relationship with the Roman Empire
- Luke had a historian's interest in finding out about the past for its own sake.

Summary

All the Evangelists, when they describe the risen Christ's meeting with his apostles, conclude with the "missionary mandate":

> The different versions of the "missionary mandate" contain common elements as well as characteristics proper to each. Two elements however are found in all the versions. First, there is the universal dimension of the task entrusted to the apostles, who are sent to "all nations" (Lk 24:47); "to the end of the earth" (Acts 1:8). Secondly, there is the assurance given to the apostles by the Lord that they will not be alone in the task, but will receive the strength and the means necessary to carry out their mission. The reference here is to the presence of the spirit and the help of Jesus himself (Mk 16:20). As for the different emphasis found in each version, Mark presents

> mission as proclamation or *kerygma* "Preach the gospel" (Mk 16:15). His aim is to lead his readers to repeat Peter's profession of faith: "You are the Christ" (Mk 8:29)...In Matthew, the missionary emphasis is placed on the foundation of the church and on her teaching (Mt 28:19–20)...In Luke, mission is presented as witness (Lk 24:48; Acts 1:8), centred especially on the Resurrection (Acts 1:22). The missionary is invited to believe in the transforming power of the gospel and to proclaim what Luke presents so well, that is conversion to God's love and mercy, the experience of a complete liberation which goes to the root of all evil, namely sin. John is the only Evangelist to speak explicitly of a "mandate," a word equivalent to "mission." He directly links the mission which Jesus entrusts to his disciples with the mission which he himself has received from the father: "As the Father has sent me, even so I send you" (Jn :21). Addressing the Father Jesus says: "As you sent me into the world, so I have sent them into the world." (Jn 17:18) [22]

The message of "Go Teach All Nations" and its meaning comes out clearly in all accounts from the New Testament. While the audiences and the writers came from different backgrounds, the message was the same even though it had to be phrased in a different manner to suit the cultural, religions and ethnic backgrounds of the diverse audiences.

RESPONSE TO GO TEACH ALL NATIONS IN THE EARLY CHURCH

It is worthwhile looking at the history of the early church in order to get a better picture of the difficulties the church had in responding to this command in Matthew 28:16–20.

A brief history of the period (AD 0–311)

Learning from the past

Some observers today suggest that the young and many supposedly educated people are not very interested in the past:

> It is foolish not to attend to the lessons of the past. While not subscribing to the view that history repeats itself we can and ought to learn from the past, provided we attend properly to its lessons...How Christians responded to past challenges can inspire our response today. By studying the reasons why Christians in the past responded as they did we may be able

to better understand ourselves and our times.' [23]

Church history can be divided into two sections:

- Internal developments dealing with doctrine, constitution, offices and ministries, religious life, worship, catechetical and liturgical developments.
- External developments dealing with the growth and spread of the church. How the church responded to and permeated social, cultural and religious life and the emergence of institutional responses to pastoral needs.

This essay on 'Go Teach All Nations' will deal mainly with the second section.

Alexander the Great had conquered Palestine and surrounding areas during his time 356–323 BC. Later the Roman Empire took over this area, as well as Carthage, Greece, Asia Minor, Syria and Egypt. The Hellenistic culture was a product of Alexander. Politically the empire was Roman but culturally it was not Greek but Hellenistic. The Roman Empire had accepted Greek both as the language of trade and discourse among the educated. The fusion of Europe and Asia on the basis of Greek culture i.e. Hellenistic, did not achieve; nor did it ever make Greeks of the Orientals. Nevertheless it transformed the east for centuries. This culture had the same attraction for those outside it as in later centuries the material order and prosperity of the Roman Empire had for the Germanic tribes beyond the frontier.

We may distinguish roughly three main religious influences in that world into which Catholicism came: [24]

- Religions of Greece and Rome
- Celtic religious in the West
- Ancient religions of the East into which the Jewish religion falls.

The Jews were only a fraction of the empire's population: "The religion of any given city then or any given family, even of the individual, would present a curiously rich diversity in which could be distinguished, strata by strata the remains of more than one religious development and conquest." [25]

Some notable aspects of early Christianity

Early christianity had several notable aspects:

Distinctively local in an age of slow communication

Missionary

The unpromising roots of Christianity based on a small state of Palestine.

Origins

From Rural Palestinian origins Christianity becomes an urban religion in early centuries. Later in medieval times it had to be replanted in rural feudal Europe.

Theological development

Heresies led to Theological development. Greeks, perhaps unduly, explored intellectual content of faith with emphasis on Creeds and dogmas. Latin Christianity offered a superior way of life and appealed to many philosophers. There was emphasis on morals and law. Christ the great law giver. Ethics and law became central.

Other differences

The Greeks emphasised the divine in Christ. Many had a problem regarding how Christ could be human. The west emphasised the humanity of Christ, some had a problem on how he could be God also.

Rapid expansion

There was a phenomenal spread of Christianity from being seen initially by outsiders as an obscure sect within Judaism. Within a few centuries Christianity became the faith of the Roman Empire and the vast majority of its inhabitants. It had also spread eastwards as far as central Asia and probably to India and Ceylon. It reached Ireland in the West.

Limited area of early Christianity

Christianity originated and developed in the Mediterranean basin which was not the only centre of civilisation at the time. Worldwide expansion only came much later. Persia resisted Christianity because it was anti Roman Empire. India and China had their own civilisations and Christianity made little or no progress in these regions in the early church period. [26]

The relationship between the Roman Empire and the Christian Church prior to Constantine

Christianity was not a lawful religion for most of this period. Persecutions were due mainly to local factors. The state only became involved directly in persecution in the third century.

Persecution and tolerance were intermittent. Christians were regarded by Rome as pagans and a threat to the legal toleration of Jews by Rome. They were also violating the law of illegal assembly.

In the first century, the inhabitants of the Roman Empire only became slowly aware of Christians. Later in Nero's time they were feared and detested. They were regarded as atheists and immoral. They became scapegoats and the state was ready to yield to local pressure to persecute.

In the second century most educated pagans wanted the Christians punished regardless. A few writers became sympathetic. The attitude was one of intellectual contempt but moral admiration. Later the more educated became less dismissive and this led to less people believing the bad propaganda of the state. In the early third century bishops were acceptable. There was more sympathy for Christians who were suffering from oppressive edicts, however, by the middle of this century there was very severe persecution by Decius which led to widespread drop out from Christianity i.e. AD 249–251.

There was further persecution by Valerian (AD 257–259). Valerian was originally tolerant. When there was widespread insecurity later on, the Christians were used as scapegoats. The church as an institution was attacked as there was a fear of Christianisation of the Roman Empire. There were many martyrs in this period. Valerian was taken prisoner in a war at the frontier and later died. His son Gallerius abrogated the edicts of his father. Property that had been confiscated was returned. Christianity became officially recognised in AD 260. There followed forty-one years of relative peace. Diocletian became emperor in AD 285 While he did good work in reorganising the empire physically and financially he felt that Christians were in his way. Another persecution followed in AD 303–304 and severe martyrdom followed. Constantine became emperor in AD 306 and persecution ended officially on 30th of April AD 311.

The Acts of the Apostles in more detail

> The Gospel tells us clearly that while Jesus proclaimed the Kingdom of God, he also inspired his apostles to spread his message throughout the world. What is important in the early church history i.e. what really interests us is knowing what were the experiences and deeds of the true believers, apostles and martyrs. The first book dealing with these is the Acts of the Apostles, written by Luke the Evangelist. Here Luke tells us about the first stages of the church in the years following the resurrection of Christ. [27]

Acts is also interesting in that it teaches us how the early communities developed through the work of the apostles and the Holy Spirit. In Acts 1:8 Jesus tells the apostles, "But you will receive power when the Holy Spirit comes upon you and you will be my witnesses in Jerusalem, throughout Judea and Samaria, even to the ends of the earth."

The Book of Acts deals with witness in Jerusalem Acts (1:1 to 8: 4); witness in Judea and Samaria in Acts (8:5 to 12:25); witness to the ends of the earth in chapters 13 to 28.

(i) Witness in Jerusalem

> After appearing to his disciples for "forty days" (1:3) the Lord tells them to wait in Jerusalem for the fulfilment of

> His promise concerning the Holy Spirit. Ten days after His ascension this promise is fulfilled as the disciples are empowered and filled with the Holy Spirit. The disciples are transformed and filled with courage to proclaim the brand new message of the resurrected Saviour. Peter's powerful sermon, like all the sermons in Acts, is built upon the resurrection, and 3000 persons respond with saving faith. After dramatically healing a man who was lame from birth, Peter delivers a second crucial message to the people of Israel resulting in thousands of additional responses. The religious leaders arrest the apostles and this gives Peter an opportunity to preach a special sermon to them.[28]

The apostles are persecuted and imprisoned because of their witness. Seven men including Stephen and Philip are chosen to help the apostles. Stephen in his defence used the Scriptures to prove that the man crucified was the Messiah. The members of the Council martyred Stephen by stoning him to death. Incidentally Paul was holding their cloaks and approved of the action. This was before his conversion.

(ii) Witness in Judea and Samaria

Philip proclaims the message of Jesus in Samaria, a people hated by the Jews, "Peter and John confirm his work and exercise their apostolic authority by imparting the Holy Spirit to these new members of the body of Christ." [29]

Saul the prosecutor was converted into Paul the apostle to the Gentiles and uses Peter to introduce the Gospel to the Gentiles. In a vision Peter realises that Christ has no barriers between Jews and Gentiles. After Cornelius and others are converted Peter convinced the Jewish believers in Jerusalem that Gentiles also had received Gods word. Even with further persecution the Church expands rapidly throughout the Roman Empire.

(iii) Witness to the ends of the earth

Starting at chapter 13, Luke focuses on Paul instead of Peter. Antioch in Syria becomes the headquarters of the Church instead of Jerusalem. All three of Paul's journeys are made from Antioch. The first in AD 48–49 concentrates on the cities of Antioch in Pisidia, Iconium, Lystra and Derbe. After this a council in Jerusalem among the apostles and elders of the church met to determine that the Gentile converts need not be subject to the Law of Moses, including areas such as circumcision.

Paul's second missionary journey in AD 50–52 went to Galatia, Macedonia and Greece mainly to the cities of Philippi, Thessalonica and Corinth. Later he returns to Jerusalem and Antioch.

Paul's third missionary journey AD 53–57 went to Ephesis mainly and also to Macedonia and Greece. He then went back to Jerusalem against advice. He was accused by Jews of bringing Gentiles into the Temple. He would have been killed only for telling them he was a Roman citizen. The Roman governor then intervened and sent Paul to Felix the Governor of Caesarea after he heard rumours of a plot to assassinate Paul. During his two-year imprisonment there Paul defends the Christian faith before Felix, Festus and Agrippa. His appeal to Caesar required a voyage to Rome where he was placed under house arrest until his trial.

Luke's aim is that the plan of salvation would go beyond Palestine, beyond the lifetime of Jesus and the lifetime of Luke's contemporaries:

> Luke presents Jesus as the central part of the plan of God's salvation, but his death would not mean the end of his saving activity. His mission of salvation would continue beyond his earthly life, through his apostles whom he directs and guides from Jerusalem to the ends of the earth. [30]

(iv) The First Community

They were faithful to the teaching of the apostles, the common life of sharing, breaking of bread and the prayers. A holy fear came up in all the people, for, many wonders and miraculous signs, were done by the apostles. Now all the believers lived together and shared all their belongings. They would sell their property and all they had and distribute the proceeds to others according to their need. Each day they met together in the temple area; they broke bread in their houses; they shared their food with great joy and simplicity of heart; they praised God and won People's favour. And every day the Lord added to their number those who were being saved. - *Acts 2:42–47*

(v) The Early Converts

In a history of Christian mission, Stephen O'Neill says that the presence of Jews in large numbers in every part of the Roman Empire was very important in the spread of Christianity: "The quest for wisdom was an ancient passion with the Greeks always in search of something new. The Synagogue offered a profound and moving wisdom apparently more ancient than that of Homer." [31]

According to Stephen O'Neill, when this group discovered they could win all that Judaism could offer and more besides, it was not too hard for them to take a further step to become Christians. These people had been well trained in the Old Testament and this made it easy for them to accept positions of leadership. Only for Luke and Paul's writings we would know very little about the early church.

The first large body of evidence outside the New Testament, the Epistles of Ignatius confirms both the validity and the continuance of the Pauline pattern. He was martyred in Rome approx AD 110. The Gospel according to John adds a lot of good theology to the church around AD 100.

(vi) The Influence of St Paul

> In reading the New Testament, it is not difficult to get the impression that only two people really mattered in the early church: Jesus himself and Paul. The stories of Jesus in the Gospels and the writings of Paul account for something like three quarters of the whole New Testament. [32]

The writings of Paul deepen our knowledge of the Gospels. He did not know Jesus but he has come to know Jesus in a different way and wishes to communicate this.

Paul's Background

Born AD 5–15, Paul's life up to the conversion is not known. The Acts are a secondary source of Paul's background. Paul's own writings are the primary source. "I am a Jew, a citizen of

Tarsus, a well known city in Cecilia," Paul boasted of his Jewish background. As a Jew, Paul was a Pharisee (Phil 3:6) and one who excelled his peers in Judaism Gal (1:14). Paul's father was a Roman citizen and so was Paul. Tarsus was a cosmopolitan place between east and west with a university where Paul studied. He spoke Aramaic and Greek. He had two names Paul and Saul—common at the time.

Paul before the Conversion

He persecuted the Church (Gal 1:13):

- In Jerusalem (Acts 8:1–3)
- And beyond (Acts 9:1–2)
- Something he believed he should do (Acts 26:9–11)

He was advancing in Judaism (Gal 1:14):

- As a Scholar trained at the feet of Gamaliel (Acts 22:3)
- Holding positions of religious power (Acts 26:12)

He was fanatical for his ancestral religions tradition (Gal 1:14):

- Proud to be a Hebrew (Ph 3:4–5)
- Proud to be a Pharisee (Ph 3:5, Acts 23:6)

Pharisees were noted for their opposition to Jesus (Matt 2:14). The conversion story occurs three times in Acts. Chapter 9 is Luke's narrative. The other two in Chapter 19 and 26 are Paul's own accounts, as written by Luke.

Paul after the Conversion

Paul had a conversion experience on the road to Damascus, "The one whom Paul so despised and whose followers he was bent on punishing was standing before him, thereby revealing his identity as Messiah and inviting Paul to believe him." [33] The power of the Damascus experience shows how important it was because Paul left all the fanaticism aside and replaced it with a fanaticism for Christ.

"The reluctance of Ananias to have anything to do with Saul despite the Lord's instruction highlights the metamorphosis of Saul from a truly fearsome prosecutor." [34] Without this conversion experience the Church would have been Jewish Christian because Paul's Christianity moved from Jewish to Gentile in a short time.

Paul's Theology

Paul developed a theology around the saving aspect of Jesus i.e. salvation is the way Paul interprets the life of Jesus, i.e. Jesus who is dead continues to live in the Church as "the body of Christ" and offers salvation.

God through Jesus continues to be with us. Paul is interested in how Christ impacts on the people and the places he visits, so Paul's theology is "Christology." Paul as a Pharisee knew Jesus was the Messiah sent by God and is God's son. Paul had insight and knowledge and a burning conviction. To Paul the church is a continuation of the person of Christ i.e. Christ in a different mode. The Church is the whole body of people united around Christ:

> Paul was a very important person in the growth of Chris-

> tianity. He was more responsible than any other for the spreading of Christianity. In a sense he laid all the foundation stones for future theology even today and despite the fact that he was a late comer to Christianity. [35]

He gave order to a common form of worship and helped people to organise Gentile Churches and gave them ideas on worship.

Paul the letter writer

The following is a summary of the more detailed account in John Drane's book, *Introduction to the New Testament.* [36] Paul wrote letters in the common style of the day and was consistent. For example, the name of the writer and to whom it was written was followed by a greeting. This was followed by a polite expression of thanks for the good health of the person to whom he was writing or to God. The main body of the letter was often in two parts, doctrinal teaching (sometimes in response to questions) followed by advice on aspects of Christian lifestyle. Next came personal news about himself or other individuals followed by greetings. After a note of exhortation, a blessing on the person he was writing to followed in his own handwriting. Finally, ancient letters often ended with a single word such as farewell:

> Paul took advantage of the major highways the Romans had built across their empire. Combined with regular sea routes, they gave ready access to all the major centres of population and these were the places Paul visited. He knew that he could never personally take the Gospel to every man

> and woman throughout the empire, but he could establish enthusiastic groups of Christians in some of the key cities, then they in turn would spread the good news into the more remote areas. [37]

The fact that Paul was single—and apparently without a family—meant he could travel more easily than the apostles who had families. Paul was a man of his time. If we are enlightened by Paul, his questions and answers are as real today as they were then—for example, marriage and chastity are still a major issues in people's lives. The second Vatican Council has an enormous number of quotations from Paul.

In reading Paul's letters today, we need to keep the following in mind: Paul never intended them to be a comprehensive account of the Christian faith. It is difficult to have a full understanding of a person whose lifestyle and general culture are not the same as our own. Nevertheless, it is not difficult to identify those elements that formed the central core of Paul's Christian beliefs.

Ministry in the early Church

The evidence for the existence of a local ministry is plentiful in later epistles of St Paul (Philippians: 1), Timothy and Titus. The Epistle to the Philippians opens with a special greeting to the bishops and deacons. Those who hold these official positions are recognised as the representatives in some sort of Church. Throughout the letter there is no mention of the "Charismata" which figures so largely in earlier epistles. We find Churches governed by hierarchical organisations of bishops (sometimes also termed presbyters and deacons). That the term bishop and presbyter are synonymous is evident from Titus 1:5–7, "I left you in Crete because I wanted you to put right what was defective and appoint elders in every town following my instructions since the overseer (or bishop) is the steward of God's house, he must be beyond reproach."

These presbyters form a corporate body (1 Timothy 4:14) and are entrusted with the twofold charge of governing the Church (1 Timothy 3:5) and of Teaching (1 Timothy 3:2, Titus 1:9). The selection of those who are to fill this post does not depend on the possession of supernatural gifts. The appointment to this office was by solemn laying-on of hands (1 Timothy 5:22).

Moral Theology in the Early Church

The influence of Scriptures is very important. God made covenants with the chosen people in the Old Testament. Sin is the breaking of that covenant "alhalla" missing the mark or failure to reach the mark i.e. a breaking of the relationship of the people with God. "I will be your God and you will be my people." In the Old Testament, God gave the people the Ten Commandments, which were really ten Commandments of love and could be summarised in "love God and love you neighbour as yourself." In the New Testament, God's relationship with the people peaked with Jesus. God's mercy became the message. Christ came to redeem us. The everlasting covenant is Jesus Christ.

Systematic Moral Theology did not develop much in the first thousand years of Christianity. The early writings took the form of letters from Bishops, homilies and commentaries on scriptures. Emphasis was put on particular virtues and obligations and the defence of Christian morality compared to Jewish, Pagan and other approaches. From Turtullian (who about AD 240), we have several works excluding the works he wrote after his defection to Montanism. Other writers such as Clement of Alexandria (d. AD 215) and his pupil Origin (d. AD 251) of the Alexandrian school attempted to create a Scriptural and Philosophical base for Christian Morality. When the persecution ended in AD 311 we find many more writings in the form of Sermons and homilies.

RESPONSE IN VATICAN II AND SUBSEQUENT DOCUMENTS

IN ORDER TO EXAMINE THE RESPONSE to 'Go Teach All Nations' in the post Vatican II period, I find it necessary to study the relevant documents from Vatican II and subsequent encyclia from the Holy See.

The principal document dealing with this topic from Vatican II is *The Decree on the Church Missionary Activity (Ad Gentes Divinitus)* on the 7th of December 1965:

> Its principal aim was as follows: it wishes to link the efforts of all the faithful, so that the people of God, following the narrow way of the cross, might everywhere spread the Kingdom of Christ, the Lord and beholder of the ages (Eccl 36:19) and prepare the way for his coming.[38]

The document *Ad Gentes* consists of six chapters containing forty-two sub-sections. On the 12th of July 1990, Pope John

Paul II published an evangelical, *Redemptoris Missio*, in which he states, "Missionary activity specifically directed to the Nation (*Ad Gentes*) appears to be waning, and this tendency is certainly not in line with the directives of the Council and of subsequent statements of the magesterium…The present document has as its goal an interior renewal of faith and Christian life…It is in commitment to all Churches universal mission that the new evangelization of Christian people will find inspiration and support."[39]

Redemtoris missio contain eight chapters and ninety-one subsections. In fact it is more than twice the number of words of *Ad Gentes Divinitus*. In effect, it seems to be an updating and expanded version of the council document, using information published in the intervening years.

Having read both documents, I first contemplated comparing both documents but decided against this. Later I contemplated writing about the entire items in *Redemptoris missio*, and again decided against this. Finally I decided to summarise the document *Redemptoris Missio* for my own benefit, since it is such a wonderful document.

A Summary of Redemptoris Missio

Chapter 1: Jesus is the only saviour

"No one comes to the father but by me." (John 10:6). Jesus is the word of God made man. Faith in Christ is directed to man's freedom. New life is a gift from God. The human person has the right to religious freedom. The Church is a sign and an instrument of salvation. Salvation in Christ is offered to all: "We cannot stop speaking about whatever we have seen and heard" (Acts 4:20)

Chapter 2: The kingdom of God

God chose to be involved with mankind through covenants (GN 9:1–17). In the course of her history, Israel comes to realise that her election has a universal meaning. (GN 2:2–5; 25; 6–8; 60:1–6; Jer 3:17; 16:19).

Jesus of Nazareth brings God's plan to fulfilment. The proclamation and establishment of Gods Kingdom are the purpose of his mission: "Jesus was sent for this purpose" (LK4:43). The kingdom of God is at hand (Mk 1:15), its coming is to be prayed for (Mt 6:10) and entry into the kingdom comes through faith and conversation (Mk1:15).

The characteristics of the kingdom and its demands are gradually revealed by Jesus. Jesus sums up the Law:

> Love one another as I have loved you (John 13:34). In the risen Christ, God's Kingdom is fulfilled and proclaimed. By raising Jesus from the dead, God has conquered death, and in Jesus he has definitely inaugurated the Kingdom. The Kingdom of God "is not of this world…is not from the world" (John 18:36). The Kingdom of God should not be translated into the Kingdom of man which is more political. The Kingdom cannot be detached either from Christ or from the Church. Certainly the Kingdom demands the promotion of human values, as well as those which can properly be called "evangelical" since they are intimately bound up with the "Good News"'[40]

The Church is effectively at the service of the Kingdom especially in her preaching, which is a call to conversion:

> It is true that the inchoate reality of the Kingdom can also be found beyond the confines of the church among people everywhere, to the extent that they have "Gospel Values" and are open to the working of the spirit who breathes when and where he wills (Jn 3:8). But it must immediately be added that this temporal dimension of the Kingdom remains incomplete unless it is related to the Kingdom of Christ present in the Church and straining towards the escatological fullness'[41]

Chapter 3: the Holy Spirit; the principal agent of Mission.

> The spirit worked through the apostles, but at the same time he was also at work in those who heard them. Through his action, the Good News takes shape in human minds and hearts and extends through history. In all of this it is the Holy Spirit who gives life.'[42]

Send forth "to the end of the earth" (Acts 1: 8):

> This is a sending forth in the Spirit, as is clearly apparent in the Gospel of John: Christ sends his own into the world, just as the Father has sent him, and to this end he gives them the spirit. Luke, for his part, closely links the witness the apostles are to give to Christ with the working of the Spirit, who will enable them to fulfil the mandate they have received.[43]

All the Evangelists, when they described the risen Christ's meeting with his apostles, conclude with the "missionary mandate." The different versions of the missionary mandate and their common elements are covered next in this document. I have already covered these in chapter 1 of my essay.

The Holy Spirit makes the whole church missionary. To live in "fraternal Communion" (*Koinonia*) means to be "of one heart and soul" (Acts 4:32), establishing fellowship from every point of view: human, spiritual and material.' [44] The Acts of the Apostles show that the mission which was first directed to Israel and later to the Gentiles develops on many levels—first the twelve apostles, then the community of believers and later the special envoys sent out to proclaim the Gospel.

The Spirit is present and active in every time and place. The presence of the Holy Spirit and his activities are universal, limited neither to space or time. Everyone is offered the possibility of sharing in the Paschal Mystery in a manner known to God. The Spirit who "flows where he wills" (Jn 3:8), who was already at work in the world before Christ was glorified... leads us to broaden our vision in order to ponder his activity in every time and place.'[45] The Church's missionary activity is only beginning. Today all Christians are called to have the same courage that inspired the missionaries of the past, and the same readiness to listen to the voice of the Spirit.

Chapter 4: The vast horizons of the mission *Ad Gentes*

"The Church was sent by Christ to reveal and communicate the love of God to all people and nations."[46] Today we have a religious situation which is extremely varied and changing. This includes new phenomena such as urbanisation, mass migration, floods of refugees, de-christianisation of ancient Christian countries and the proliferation of missionary cults and religious sects. All Catholics should be missionaries but some persons have a specific vocation to be "life long missionaries *Ad Gentes*."

In evangelising there are three situations;

- Parishes, groups and socio cultural contexts where Christ and his Gospel are not known. This is missio *Ad Gentes.*
- The Christian communities with adequate and solid ecclesial structures.
- Intermediate situations especially in countries with ancient Christian roots and occasionally in younger churches where entire groups of baptised have lost a living sense of faith or even no longer consider themselves members of the church. This situation needs evangelization or a new evangelization.

Mission activity proper, or mission *Ad Gentes,* is directed at people or groups who do not yet believe in Christ. This mission work must always be distinguishable from the others; on the other hand the boundaries between groups are not clearly definable. Traditional Christian countries are coming to understand the difficulty of being missionaries to non-christian countries in far away places if they are not seriously concerned about the non-Christians at home.

The mission *Ad Gentes* is to all people in spite of all the difficulties. The task is out of proportion to the Church's human resources.

Examples of difficulties are; refusal of entry, refusal to evangelize, refusal of Christian worship. In some places conversion is seen as a rejection of ones own people and Culture.

Lack of fervour can be manifested in fatigue disenchantment, compromise, lack of interest and lack of hope. There can also be divisions amongst Christians; one of the most serious reasons for lack of interest in the missionary task is widespread indifferentism, which is found also among Christians.

Due to Christ's universal mandate, the human *Ad Gentes* has no boundaries. Missionary activity *Ad Gentes* is measured within well defined territories and groups of people. Many areas have not been reached even in traditionally Christian countries—for example, in Asia, Christians are a small minority.

The southern hemisphere where before there were stable human and social situations, is under pressure due to urbanisation and the massive growth of cities. In many countries one half of the population live in megalopolies where human problems are often aggravated by the feeling of anonymity experienced by masses of people.

Today the mission *Ad Gentes* is more concentrated in big cities. The future of young nations is being shaped in the cities. The young people in these countries are over half the population. Migration has produced new phenomena. Non-Christians are increasing rapidly in traditionally Christian countries. On the positive side this creates opportunities for contacts and cultural exchanges. The Church must make refugees part of her overall apostolic concern. St Paul spoke in the *Areopagus* which represented the cultural centre of the learned people of Athens. This is a symbol of the new sections in which the Gospel must be proclaimed. The *Areopagus* of the modern age is world communications which is becoming the "global village." The young generation are being conditioned by mass media. Using the media simply to spread the Christian message is not enough:

> This is a complex issue since the "new culture" originates not just from whatever content is eventually expressed, but from the very fact that there exists new ways of communicating with new languages, new technology and a new psychology. [47]

Other forms of *Areopagus are*: commitment to peace, development and liberation of peoples, the rights of individuals and people especially minorities, the advancement of women and children, safeguarding the created world. These areas need to be illuminated also with the light of the Gospel. Also there are the *Areopagus* of Culture, Scientific research and International relations:

> Religious freedom, which is still at times restricted, remains the promise and guarantee of all the freedoms that ensure the common good of individuals and people.[48]

Pope Benedict xv already cautioned the missionaries of his time lest they forget their proper dignity and think more of their earthly homeland than their heavenly one. In directing attention towards the south and the East, the fact remains that the "Ends of the Earth" to which the Gospel refers are growing more distant. The mission *Ad Gentes* is still in its infancy. The number of people in the South and the East who remain unaware of Christ's redemption is increasing not decreasing.

Chapter 5: The paths of Mission

The emphasis here is teaching by example: "Missionary activity is nothing other and nothing less than the manifestation or epiphany of Gods plan and its fulfilment in the world and in history."[49] The first form of Evangelization is witness. People today put more trust in witness, experience and life and action than in teaching, teachers and theories. Proclamation is the permanent priority of mission. The Good News of their being loved and saved by God should not be deprived to anyone.

Initial proclamation has a key role, as it introduces man "into the mystery of the Love of God, who invites him to enter into a personal relationship with himself in Christ." [50] There exists in people an expectation—even if an unconscious one—of knowing the truth about God and how we are to be set free from sin and death.

Conversion is a gift of God, a work of the blessed trinity (John 6:44): "No one can come to me unless the Father who sent me draws him." Conversion means accepting, the saving sovereignty of Christ and becoming his disciple. The apostles invited all to change their lives to be converted and to be baptised. In formation of local Churches it is conversion and baptism which leads to the establishing of the local communities which leads to the formation of local churches. The objectives of *Ad Gentes* are to format Christian communities and develop churches to their full maturity.

There are many areas with no churches or an insufficient number for the population. The universal church must contribute. By being a missionary church, it will overcome internal divisions. "The good shepherd who devotes himself to the flock, but at the same time is mindful of the other sheep that are out in this fold" (John 10:16). This is also a stimulus for a renewed commitment to ecumenism: "The fact that the Good News of reconciliation is preached by Christians who are divided among themselves weakens their witness." [51]

It is true that some kind of communion, though imperfect, exists among all those who have received baptism in Christ:

> Catholics should collaborate in a spirit of fellowship with their separate brothers and sisters in accordance with the norms of the decree on Ecumenism; by a common profession of faith in God and in Jesus Christ before the nations—to the extent that this is possible and by their cooperation in social and technical as well as in cultural and religious matters.[52]

Ecclesial basic communities as a form for Evangelization

This encyclical approves of the new basic communities, if they truly live in unity with the church, which are a true expression of communion and a means for the construction of a more profound communion: "They are thus cause for great hope for the life of the church." [53] These are groups of Christians who at the level of the family, or in a similarly restricted setting, come together for prayer, Scripture reading, catechism, and discussion on human and ecclesial problems with a view to a common commitment.

Incarnating the Gospel in people's culture

> Inculturation means the intimate transformation of authentic cultural values through their integration in Christianity and the insertion of Christianity in the various human cultures. Through inculturation the church, for her part, becomes a more intelligible sign of what she is, and a more effective instrument of mission. [54]

Missionaries must become involved in the culture, language and live with the people without renouncing their own cultural identity. As a consequence the ecclesial communities will gradually improve their Christian experience in original ways and forms that are in harmony with their own cultural tradition. During this process, the Bishops as guardians of the flock will be a great help: "Inculturation must involve the whole people of God, and not just a few experts, since the people reflect the authentic senses fidei which must never be lost sight of." [55]

Dialogue with our brothers and sisters of other religions

> The fact that the followers of other religions can receive God's grace and be saved by Christ apart from the ordinary means which he has established does not thereby cancel the call of faith and baptism which God wills for all people.[56]

Dialogue is a ray of hope which enlightens all men. Dialogue is based on hope and love, and will bear fruit in the Spirit. Other religions provide a positive challenge for the church as well as the opportunity to examine more deeply her own identity. Proper dialogue must be without pretence or closed-mindedness, but with truth, humility and frankness, knowing that dialogue can enrich each side, without abandonment of principles. Each member of the faithful and all Christian communities are called to practice dialogue although not always to the same degree or in the same way.

Promoting development by forming consciences

Today, more than in the past, missionaries are being recognised as promoters of development by governments and international experts who are impressed at the remarkable results achieved with scarce means:

> It is not the churches mission to work directly on the economic, technical or political levels, or to contribute materially to development. Rather her mission consists essentially in offering people an opportunity not to "have more" but to "be more" by awakening their conscience through the Gospel. Authentic human development must be rooted in an even deeper evangelisation.[57]

There is a close connection between proclamation of the Gospel and human promotion. The church and evangelisation has helped people in their struggle against poverty and under-development in the southern hemisphere. It can also help people of the northern hemisphere where there is over-development. An excess of affluence can be as harmful as an excess of poverty. There is a development model which the north has constructed and is now spreading to the south, where a sense of religion as well as human values are in danger of being overwhelmed by a wave of consumerism. "Fight hunger by changing your lifestyle" is a motto which has appeared in church circles, which shows the people of the rich nations how to become brothers of the poor. [58]

Charity: Sources and Criterion of Mission

The church wishes to be the church of the poor and to draw on the truth contained in the Beatitudes of Christ, especially "Blessed are the poor in Spirit." She wishes to teach the truth and put it into practice, just as Jesus came to do and teach.

The Pope wishes to thank all the priests, religious brothers and sisters, and members of the Laity for their dedication, and also the volunteers from non government organisations for their dedication.

Chapter 6: Leaders and Workers in the Missionary Apostolate.

Without witnesses there is no witness, without missionaries there is no missionary activity. Peter, James and John were leaders among the apostles and the way was prepared for the outstanding missionary work of Paul. Others should not be ignored, such as the local church of Antioch who became an evangelising community, sending out missionaries. Young churches should get involved in the universal mission as soon as possible—as recommended in *Ad Gentes* 20. Older churches should draw from the riches of younger churches and vice versa.

The primary responsibility for missionary activity

This document claims that the Bishops are directly responsible for the evangelization of the world. There must be cooperation among churches especially in regard to distribution of clergy: "Those who have received this vocation sent by legitimate authority, go out, in faith and obedience, to those who are far from Christ, set aside for the work which they have been called as ministers of the Gospel." [59] Today missionary institutes are receiving more candidates from young churches which they founded and new missionary institutes have arisen in countries which previously only received missionaries but are now also sending them.

Diocesans Priests for the Universal Mission

> The spiritual gift that priests have received in ordination prepares them, not for any narrow and limited mission, but for the most universal and all embracing mission of salvation to the end of the earth: for every priestly ministry shares in the universal scope of the mission that Christ entrusted to his apostles.[60]

Missionary fruitfulness of consecrated life

A special word of thanks is extended to religious families and to the missionary sisters "in the spread of faith and the formation of new churches." [61]

All Laity are missionaries by Baptism

> The mission *Ad Gentes* is incumbent upon the entire people of God. Whereas the foundation of a new church requires the Eucharist and hence the priestly ministry, missionary activity, which is carried out in a wide variety of ways, is the task of all Christian faithful.[62]

> Within missionary activity, the different forms of lay apostolate should be held in esteem, with respect for their nature and aims. Lay missionary associations, international Christian volunteer organisations, ecclessical movements, groups and solidarities if different kinds—all these should be involved in the mission *Ad Gentes.* [63]

The work of Catechists and the variety of ministries

Missionaries are very dependent on Catechists. They represent the basic strength of Christian communication especially in young churches. It is important to establish support schools for Catechists which are approved and confer accreditation such as diplomas.

Other church personnel such as leaders of prayer, song and liturgy, Ecclesial Communities and Bible Study groups, charitable works, administration of resources, religion teachers in schools are also important:

> Leaders and agents of missionary pastoral activities should sense their unity within the communion which characterises the Mystical Body (John 17:21): "Even as you, father, are in me, and I in you, that they also be in us, so that the world may believe that you have sent me." The fruitfulness of missionary activity is to be found in the communion. [64]

I can only confirm these wise directives. In order to re-launch the mission *Ad Gentes*, a centre of outreach, direction and coordination is needed—namely the congregation of the Evangelisation of Peoples. [65] The leaders and institutions involved in missionary activity should join forces and initiatives as opportunities suggest.

Chapter 7: Cooperation in Missionary Activity

All Christians share responsibility for missionary activities. Only if we are united in Christ (John 15:5) can we produce good fruit.

Prayer and Sacrifice for Missionaries

In his letters, St. Paul often asked people to pray for him, so he might proclaim the Gospel with confidence and conviction. Prayer needs to be accompanied by sacrifice; the solemnity of Pentecost is celebrated in some communities as "A Day of Suffering for the mission's." (Is 6:8) "Here I am Lord! I am Ready! Send me!" Cooperation is expressed above all by promoting vocations. Parents should foster missionary vocations among their sons and daughters. Acts 20:35 "It is more blessed to give than to receive." Finance is needed for Churches, schools, Catechists, Seminarians, housing and charitable works, education and human promotion. World mission day should be an important day in the life of the church.

The forms of missionary cooperation

New activities demand cooperation e.g. visits to missions by young people, immigration by non Christians. Also, this can include cooperation in regard to politics, economics, culture and journalism. There is an increasing interdependence between people.

Missionary promotion and formation among the People of God

Missionary formation is the task of the local church, assisted by missionaries and their institutes, and by personnel from the young churches. [66] Modern technology should be used to form and inform the people of God to share in the churches universal mission.

The primary responsibility of the Pontifical Mission Societies

- Propagation of the faith
- St Peter the Apostle
- Holy Childhood and Missionary Union
- The Missionary Union

These have a common purpose of fostering a universal missionary spirit among the people of God—not only giving to the missions but receiving from them as well. It is by giving generously that we will receive. Young churches can be in a position to send priests to older churches. God is preparing a new Springtime for the Gospel. Today there is a new consensus among peoples about the values contained in the Gospels such as the rejection of violence and war; respect for human persons and human rights and desire for freedom; justice and brotherhood; surmounting racism and nationalism and affirming the dignity and role of women.

Chapter 8: Missionary Spirituality

Being led by the Spirit

It was the Spirit that transformed the apostles into courageous witnesses for Christ, and guided them along the difficult and new paths of mission. Today we must allow ourselves to be led by the Spirit also.

Living the mystery of Christ the one who was sent

An essential characteristic of missionary spirituality is the intimate communion with Christ. We must refer to Christ as the one sent to evangelize: "The missionary is required to renounce himself and everything that up to this point he considered as his own, and to make himself everything to everyone."[67]

Loving the church and humanity as Jesus did

"Those who have the missionary spirit feel Christ's burning love for souls, and love the church as Christ did." [68]

The true missionary is the saint

The universal call to holiness is linked to the universal call to mission. Every member of the church is called to both. The church's missionary Spirituality is a journey toward holiness:

> Dear brothers and sisters: let us remember the missionary enthusiasm of the first Christian communities. Despite limited means of travel and communication the proclamation of the gospel quickly reached the ends of the earth.[69]

Underlying this missionary dynamism was the holiness of the first Christians, and first communities. The future of mission depends to a great extent on contemplation. Unless the missionary is a contemplative he cannot proclaim Christ in a credible way: "In a world tormented and oppressed by so many problems , a world tempted to pessimism ,the one who proclaims the "Good News" must be a person who has found true hope in Christ." [70]

Pope John Paul's address of 20/1/2001

I am including here some extracts from an address by Pope John Paul II in 2001 and from the Catholic bishops of the USA in 2005.

Missionary activity is more necessary than ever:

> Bearing all this in mind, from the beginning of my pontificate I invited every person and people to open the doors to Christ. This missionary concern has spurred me to make many apostolic journeys, to give an ever greater role of missionary openness to the entire activity of the apostolic see and to foster constant doctrinal reflection on the apostolic task that belongs to every baptized person. The encyclical *Redemptoris Missio*, whose 10th anniversary we are celebrating, arose in this context.
>
> When I published this encyclical 10 years ago, it was the 25th anniversary of the approval of the second Vatican council's Missionary Decree *Ad Gentes*. In a certain way, then, this encyclical could be considered a commemoration of the entire Council whose purpose was to make the church's message more understandable and her pastoral activity more effective for spreading Christ's salvation in our times...On closer sight, then, the mission ad gentes has become necessary everywhere in recent years, because of rapid, massive migrations that are bringing non-Christian groups to regions with an established Christian tradition.[71]

Statement by the USA Conference of Bishops in 2005

The following are extracts from a more recent document, approved by the United States conference of catholic bishops in 2005

Teaching the Spirit of Mission Ad Gentes: Continuing Pentecost Today

The great call of apostleship

The apostles were told to go *Ad Gentes*–that is "to all nations," to those who did not know Christ, and to proclaim the gospel. However this mission is far from complete. There are many young churches that need missionaries to develop and grow. There are many diocese, eparchies, and countries struggling with poverty persecution, war, and immense suffering that need missionaries to witness to the light and love of Christ, bringing hope for the future. [72]

World mission and teaching ministry

We are enormously grateful for the devotion and skill with which Catholics in the ministry lead the way:

- *Catechists*
- *Directors of religious education*
- *Priests, religious and deacons*
- *Adult education directors*
- *Youth and young adult ministers*
- *Campus ministers*
- *Teachers and administrators in Catholic schools and institutes of higher education*

- *Seminary professors and instructors*
- *Mission office directors*

We call on everyone with teaching roles to guide the faithful towards a renewed fervour in spreading the Good News by witness and word. [73]

A word of encouragement

In an *ad limina* address to a group of bishops in 2004, Pope John Paul II appealed to the Church in the United States to recapture its missionary spirit. The bishop's statement continues, "We look to Christ himself as the model of the truly loving missionary."[74] The ultimate purpose of mission is to enable people to share in the communion that exists between the father and the son (Redemptoris 23). God "wills everyone to be saved and to come to knowledge of the truth" (1 Timothy 2:4)

Eucharistic Sustenance

Missionaries carry with them the word and sacrament: "The same message of Christ that was passed on to the apostles, missionaries now pass on to others." [75]

An invitation to know Christ

> In this age of extreme moral and religious relativism, Christ's mission to the world has become more difficult but even more necessary. Mission is never an imposition upon the free will of another; it is an invitation to know Christ or to know him better, and it is made in a spirit of respect toward others. Missionaries deeply desire all peoples throughout

> the world to share in the riches of Christ and his Church.[76]

The fire of the Holy Spirit

> We bishops, as diocesan leaders and successors of the very first apostles—and all those who teach the faith, as Christ's witnesses—are all disciples, sent by Christ to preach the Gospel to every corner of the earth.[77]

Mission and the global community

Mission while happily making use of technological advances in communications, is still very much a person-to- person ministry:

> We applaud all that is good in the idea of the global community, which in its highest form represents a desire for peace and community throughout the world. We also recognize that our Catholic faith needs to confront those ideas that are perilous. Other values that degrade the human spirit are also promoted worldwide today: extreme secularism, relativism, individualism, and consumerism—all of which drive people further apart. They are contrary to the Gospel of Christ and to all that is good.[78]

Inter-religious Dialogue and Mission

> How do Catholics lovingly proclaim faith in Christ while respecting the differing faiths of those they encounter? This is done through "inter-religious dialogue," and by living our faith in Christ. While we always invite others to the Catholic faith, we also strive to understand—and value—what is positive in their beliefs. This work is done both by missionaries abroad and by us at home.
>
> On the basis of trust built through love, all Catholics reach

out as missionaries and confidently announce the Good News of Christ with words and deeds. The best Christian testimony is love for others.[79]

Teaching Missionaries: Fostering the Missionary Spirit through Education

There are many ways to accomplish this: forming a network of concern and prayer for missions; inviting others to consider becoming missionaries; encouraging others to support missions with financial contributions. [80]

Mission in the Parish

Mission education must take place both in the family and in the parish. It is in the family that true Christian minds are first formed, and in the parish that families grow in faith. There are many rich opportunities to teach about mission in the parish:

- Religious education formation programs
- All sacramental preparation programs, especially Baptism and Confirmation
- The invitation to local missionaries or priests from overseas to visit parishes and schools
- The publication of missionary stories
- The teaching of mission histories, such as the study and reflection on the lives of co-patron saints of the Church's worldwide missionary work, St. Francis Xavier and St Thérèse of Lisieux, and a great missionary of modern times, Blessed Mother Teresa Of Calcutta.
- The commemoration of the martyred missionaries

and persecuted churches throughout the world, which brings to mind the Passion, Death, and Resurrection of Jesus Christ' [81]

World Mission Sunday

This celebration, offered in the context of the Eucharist (see Redemptoris Missio, no. 81), is an opportunity for teachers to promote the mission spirit in parishes:

- Children can read about mission and report on it to classes.
- Contacts can be made with missionaries for World Mission Sunday.
- Bible studies and sharing groups can focus on passages dealing specifically with mission.
- A fund-raising project for world missions and mission churches can be launched.'[82]

Parish Twinning

Whole parishes can become interested and form bonds with a mission parish. This could be undertaken under the approval of the local bishop.

In conclusion the first mission Sunday was Pentecost and the mission ends at the end of time, i.e. the end of Christ's mission on earth.

RESPONSE IN TODAY'S MINISTRY

This chapter deals with a number of main areas of interest: a survey of Irish missionary personnel overseas; a summary of the missionary work of one congregation in particular; examples of Irish Catholic missionary work in 3 continents; an examination of youth as a source of a response (based on a survey of youth in two Irish towns); and finally, recent progress compared to the early Church.

A survey of Irish missionary personnel overseas in 2004

This survey represents the figures as of 1/6/2004.These figures are updated every two years. There were 2387 people from Ireland involved in overseas Catholic mission working in 90 countries, in Africa, Asia/Oceania, Latin America/Caribbean and Middle East/Eastern Europe. Approximately 107 Societies and organisations are involved.

In Africa there are 1477 personnel in 32 countries compared to 1651 in 35 countries in 2002. Omitted from this survey are the following:

- Priests and the religious who belong to organisations with no base in Ireland
- Development workers who work for less than two years
- Priests and religious in Western Europe, Faeroe Islands, Iceland ,North America, New Zealand, Australia.

The following are excerpts from this survey:

The Percentage of Irish Catholic Missionaries in different Continents [83]

Africa	62%
Asia / Oceania	20%
Latin America / Caribbean	16%
Middle East / Eastern Europe	2%

Note: These figures are arrived at from the numbers in each continent.

Priests accounted for 45% of Irish Catholic missionaries[84]

Sisters	47%
Brothers	7%
Laity	1%

Analysis of Catholic Missionary Activity [85]

Activity	Personnel involved
Pastoral	44%
Education	16.4%
Health	7.4%
Community Development / Social Work	6%
Administration	5.9%
Formation / Renewal	8%
Other ministries	2.6%
Retired	9.7%

Note: These figures are arrived at by adding the number of personnel in each activity from all the societies involved.

A summary of the missionary work of one Congregation

I am using the following as an example of the missionary work of one congregation (The Congregation of the Holy Spirit):

> The nettle was grasped by Pope John XXIII when he called the second Vatican Council, which accepted that the basic truth and identity of the Christian revelation could only remain living and relevant to the many changing cultures of our world, if the expression of that revelation was meaningful to the cultures addressed.[86]

This change brought about division, in the congregation, and in the Irish province of the congregation of the Holy Spirit. Added to the trauma caused by this change was the quite rapid reduction in the number of members belonging to the province and the ageing of the membership. The average number of ordinations per year dropped from 23 in the 1960s to one or two in the 1990s. It would seem to be a time to draw the wagons in a circle, nurse the wounds caused by the division, reduce commitments and carefully nurture the remnant.

> Instead what we have seen happening over the last thirty years is an explosion of creativity and many new initiates. There has been an extraordinary expansion rather than careful entrenchment. The outbreak of the Biafran war took a block of 30 Irish Spiritans out of Nigeria. This meant that the local church had to fend for themselves which they did magnificently. It also made available many experienced missionaries for other missions, which they undertook with great courage and very beneficial effect. Thus the mission spread to Papua New Guinea, Australia, Zambia, Malawi, South Africa, Ghana, Ethiopia, Mexico and to parts of the U.S.A, and England.
> Meanwhile initiatives were being undertaken in the older Spiritan missions, like Kenya, Sierra Leone, Gambia and Brazil, to encourage holistic human development send to awaken local vocations to the priestly and religious life, swell as train the laity for various leadership roles. [87]

In the present era of mission, leadership has been much

more collective, expressed in shared reflection and discussion. Chapters, Councils, Commissions, meetings and discussions of all kinds, seminars, workshops, and courses have assumed great prominence and have been the sources of the initiatives we have seen. Missionary activity has been driven by shared reflection and team-work:

> In the first half of the 20th century most people saw the church as Europe with some outlying missions. Now the world has become one Global Village, due to the extraordinary development in communications of all sorts. The church too is becoming a Global Church with autonomous local churches (rather than missions) everywhere. [88]

> The Holy Spirit is the ultimate director of mission. Under the Spirit's powerful yet subtle guidance, the present era of mission is as wonderful and as worthy of thanksgiving as any in the history of the province. [89]

In the 2004 survey of Irish Personnel overseas, the congregation of the Holy Spirit had 88 missionaries in 23 countries as defined by that survey. [90]

Examples of Irish Catholic Missionary work

The following are six examples out of the many I researched which illustrate how the missionary statement of "Go Teach All Nations" has been applied by Irish missionaries in three continents.

Celebrating Excellence

Dublin born Divine Word Missionary Andy Campbell was recently honoured as Ghana's Foreign Personality of the decade. The announcement was made at the Second Millennium Excellence awards ceremony in the capital, Accra.

The chairman of the Lepers' Aid Committee was commended as "a noble foreigner who has in the last decade stood tall among Ghanaians, contributed significantly to the development of the nation and excelled in his chosen career through his unparalleled competence and selfless devotion to duty."

UN Secretary General Kofi Annan was among the other 26 recipients to receive awards from the president of Ghana in recognition of his championing of the cause of peace. [91]

Significant People

Fr. Richard Griffin talks about significant people he met on his mission work. One such person was the old man Lemokirion:

> He and his extended family lived about three kilometres from our mission house. Their home was a series of igloo-shaped huts: branches covered with skins and pieces of plastic. I frequently went on my motorbike to visit them. We would sit and chat and pray a little. The thrill for the children was a quick ride on the motorbike around the compound. Lomokirion had an important function to perform in our main parish church on Sundays and major feast days. Before the priest's blessing at the end of mass, he also would be invited to bless the people. This he did with real gusto, calling down in his own native language the blessings of God and

> of their ancestors on all the people and their animals. The blessing took the form of a chant and response: the whole congregation playing their part. Lomokirion reminded me of an Old Testament figure, a Moses type figure. I remember his faith, his leadership, and his love of his people. [92]

News from Lare, Kenya

Br. Brian Johnson is a Franciscan brother working in Kenya and mentions the following in his recent letter to me:

> It was a mixed year here in Lare. Our blessings came in the form of a fairly good harvest, adequate rainfall, new classrooms and good school results. Our sadness comes from the many young people that continue to die from HIV/AIDS. Our school building project continues and is on schedule. As I write we are digging the foundation for our new library. The library will not only be a school library but will be a library for the wider community in which we will have adult education activities. Four classrooms and a staff room are completed and occupied. They are simple and beautiful and most appreciated by students, staff and parents.
>
> Our school continues to excel despite the many hardships and lack of electricity. Our results from last year's Kenya Certificate of Secondary Education are the best ever. We have more students eligible for university and third level institutions than in any previous year. Our extra effort in recruiting girls can be seen in the record number of girls applying to third level institutions. (Girls in our community do not normally go to secondary school.)
>
> Last year we started a program of Alternative Rites of Pas-

sage for young men and women. Instead of being mutilated by some of the traditionalists we decided to hold our own Alternative Initiation Rites. The male rite of passage (circumcision) is conducted by a qualified medical team and the girls are spared the horrors of Female Genital Mutilation. The girls go through all the rites, rituals and customs except the "cut."

This is our response to seeing several of our young boys and girls die or be severely disabled.

Archbishop Michael Courtney in Burundi

Michael Courtney was from Nenagh, Co. Tipperary. He was murdered outside Bunjumbura in Burundi in East Africa on December 29th, 2003. He had been due to go to a new appointment as Apostolic Nuncio to Cuba but asked for permission to remain for a further month in Burundi as he felt he was close to achieving a peace accord in the country, where over 300,000 people had been killed in ten years. The peace accord which resulted largely from his efforts is still tentatively holding. I met him on one occasion when he was home from Cuba where he previously worked. He mentioned the difficulty in speaking out against the Government in Cuba.

The number of Catholics killed on missions in 2005 was 25, almost double that of the previous year. The list include missionary's *Ad Gentes* and also other church personnel who sacrificed their lives. We are asked to remember all these people in our prayers.

Fr. Dan's Christmas message 2005

Rev. Fr. Dan Fitzgerald is in his eighties and still working in the Nenagh parish. He was previously a Columban missionary in China. The following is an extract from his recent Christmas message:

> The memory of Christmas 1948 when the Communist guerrilla forces controlled most of central China and there was only one country parish in which it was possible to have the Christmas Mass. A year later the diocese was part of communist China and we were living under a regime that was putting into practice Marxist Leninist theory and ideology, with its basic principle of class warfare. We had a small community of Loreto sisters who had a middle school for girls between the ages of 14 and 16, most of them non-Christians. The students had been attending induction meetings every week. They had been told that the relationship between themselves and the sisters was too friendly, and at a meeting of students from all second level schools they had been told that they must learn to hate the sisters because all reactionaries would have to be liquidated eventually. I always remember Christmas day 1949, going with the bishop to visit the sisters who were very frightened by the reports brought back by the students. The bishop, of course, was quite anxious. We went into the convent chapel. At both sides of the alter there were scrolls hanging on the walls of the sanctuary with the message of the angels in Chinese characters—"Glory to God in the highest, and on earth peace to men of good will." We said a prayer and then started to walk back to the bishop's compound. We walked in silence but from time to time, the bishop would say to himself, "Yes, yes indeed, peace on earth to men of good will." The spirit of darkness

was so different from the spirit of light. [93]

The Bible in Brazil

"It is mostly poor people, some illiterate, who are in the bible groups. Nearly every Catholic family has a bible in Brazil, where it is now the backbone of the Church." [94] Fr. Tom Hughes joined the Divine Word Missionaries 42 years ago. He is now based in Curitiba and is co-ordinator of the SVD biblical work in Brazil. A Japanese born priest Fr. Shigeyuki had started bible courses earlier: "We had 450 bible groups in the 55 churches of the parish, which was 45 miles long by 12 miles wide and had about 45000 people. Then around 1988 our southern Brazilian Province set up a bible centre for our biblicate apostolate, and that's how I became involved." [95] The biblical apostolate grew from the basic communities. Fr. Mestres, a Carmelite, gave it form and consistency in the late 1960's.

"It is mainly poor people in rural areas who are in the bible groups," explains Tom. "In most rural areas about 80% of the people don't have Mass every Sunday, due to the shortage of priests."

"They have an hour long prayer service instead. How are these rural bible group meetings run? They begin with a prayer, then they reflect on some aspects of their own lives or a real-life situation. We supply them with small booklets, which refer them to an appropriate text in the bible. They discuss what this means for them today and how best they can learn from it. The meetings are structured and also end with prayers. For millions of poor people across Brazil who take part, their only knowledge of the bible is from hearing it read—mainly the New Testament, but also the Old, especially Exodus, the prophets, and the Psalms." [96]

World Aid Nenagh support for Missions

In 2004 they donated €31,000 to 51 missionaries excluding the Tsunami Appeal which came to €85,000

An Examination of Youth as a Source of a Response

A survey of Youth in two Irish Towns

> Many in the Church today believe that we are on the verge of losing the most important social group for renewal: young people. The evangelization of youth is seen today as a question of life and death for the Church. But people are confused. Parents are perplexed and in a pained tone of voice ask "where did I go wrong?" They feel guilty because they have not been as successful as their own parents in handing on the faith to their children. Church leaders, religious educators, catechists and youth ministers are also perplexed as they search for the key for motivating and involving today's youth...[97]

I am including information from two recent surveys on youth, from a parish in South Tipperary in Waterford diocese and a town in North Tipperary, in Killaloe diocese

Highlights of the survey from St Nicholas' Parish, Carrick-on-Suir, 2005

33% attend Mass every week
45% attend Mass once a year
5% have not attended Mass in the last 3 years
90% believe in Heaven
28% believe in hell
28% believe that Jesus is God.
50% believe that Jesus came to save them.
85% accept the occasional value of prayer
79% have spoken to a priest at least once in the previous year.
85% thought parents always or at least often were prepared to listen to them.
2% thought parents never listen to them
54% thought priests were prepared to listen to them
5% thought priests never listen to them
20% thought teachers were prepared to listen to them
16% thought teachers never listen to them.
10% thought politicians were prepared to listen to them
44% thought politicians never listen to them.

The input from participants, especially in the follow up sessions, was serious and thought provoking. Very little negative feedback was noticed. Most have a very real, if misunderstood connection with the church...They are far from lost, and might best be referred to, to paraphrase the poet Milton, as hungry sheep who look up and are not fed.[98]

The majority would get married in a church and would

have their children baptized. A majority would be interested in a Youth Pastoral Council run by young people and listened to by others—not used simply as recruiting ground for readers and servers.

Some Extracts from a survey of 163 young people 15 to 18 years old (Nenagh) in 2002
Note: In this survey students were randomly selected from 3 post primary schools.

> 88% have taken alcohol in the 15 to 17 age group.
> 17% have taken drugs other than alcohol or cigarettes on a regular basis.
> 33% of females and 12% of males are not involved in extra-curricular activities. If they are not involved in extracurricular activities, young people often have no option but to hang around the town, probably outside a café or fast food restaurant, because of a lack of alternatives.
> Young people consider the town an environment that is not able to fulfil their needs for self expression and where the activities on offer are dominated by competitive sports. Only the best get ahead (or on the team).[99]

In 2004 many meetings were held in Nenagh to discuss the Diocesan Pastoral Plan. Many important topics were discussed including youth. As a consequence 6000 signatures were collected for the provision of a Youth Officer for the town. A Youth club was established for 12 to 15 year olds with 60 members. A Youth Officer was subsequently appointed and funded by the government.

It is hoped that some of these youth will take a more active role in the life of the church in the future. A continuing project in Zambia, where a number of CBS students work each summer is very encouraging.

The key to understanding young people today

In *The Pastoral Challenge of a New Age*, George Boran reminds us that the minds and values of young people are shaped by modern culture. Therefore, an understanding of modern culture is the key to understanding young people and helping them on the road to Christian values and commitment. He feels that we may be on the brink of losing a generation. It is not that young people attack the church. People who fight with the church are still interested. Something worse is happening. Young people are leaving the institution and are indifferent to its message:

> Experts have observed that, today, two generations are sufficient for people to lose any sense of real contact with Christianity. When the first generation decide not to practise or educate its children in the faith, the second generation has no faith reference. Some may return to the church for cultural reasons, to participate in a wedding or Mass. [100]

Before, a traditional culture favoured faith. This culture has changed. It was easy to believe when everyone believed. It was a matter of following the tide. Now there is a different culture—a modern culture that pushes religion to the margins. The tide has changed. To believe, one must swim against the tide. In this chapter George Boran also discusses the importance of Symbols, Myths and Ritual.

In previous generations major cultural changes have taken hundreds of years to occur. Today, many of us have passed through three major cultural shifts in our lifetime: Premodern, modern and postmodern. Vatican II attempts to pass from a medieval culture to a modern culture. Some sections have not passed over this bridge yet. In writing about post modern culture, Boran deals with globalisation, a more holistic approach to reasoning, formation through image versus reading, criticism of the myth of unlimited progress, the difficulties with permanent commitment, the shift from a collective to a private idea, an eventual return to the sacred.

Postmodern culture recognises that the goal of unlimited material growth is unreal. The resources of the earth are limited. A part of the planet can live in luxury and waste at the expense of the other part. This is really cultural reality for slow learners.

Finally, George Boran discusses his fourteen pastoral solutions for the new millennium which are worthy of further study in the future.

Recent progress compared to the Early Church

Essentially the two moments in history are very similar. The proposals that Vatican II had in mind were the "back to basics" that the church saw in the early church. Acts is the basic text for a glimpse into the life of the early Christian church. In the first few chapters we see the community in Jerusalem in prayer, sharing, the teaching of the apostles, celebrating the Eucharist. "Prayer" was almost exclusively for the Christians in Jerusalem, the Jewish liturgy in the temple (remember the Psalm "seven times a day, I will praise you O Lord"). Thus in the post resurrection period, Christianity was essentially seen as a sect of Judaism, up to the time of the destruction of the temple.

Today the smaller celebrations of the Eucharest, the New Catechetical Way, and the new Ecclesial movements are all a series of initiatives to return to the intimacy that the early church had. The Vatican II decree on the liturgy, *Sacrosanctum Concilium* recalls this, and seeks to renew the liturgical life of prayer in the church, rather than, as it had become in the intervening years. "The council also desires that, where necessary, the rites be revised carefully in the light of sound tradition, and that they be given new vigour to meet present–day circumstances and needs." [101] There is a fundamental conviction that the church has a contribution to make in every aspect of the life of the world, and that the early church was a model of how the church should be in the modern world.

The Diocesan Pastoral Plan

A good example of a new development that is happening in the church is the Diocesan Pastoral Plan:

> Since the publication of the Killaloe plan in 2004, very significant work has been done in a variety of areas across the diocese. Among the initiatives taken are the continuing formation of the clergy, participation by parents and parish in the preparation of children for First Communion and Confirmation, improving Sunday Eucharist Liturgies and paraliturgies, development of prayer groups, implementation of Child Protection Guidelines, co-operation between neighbouring parishes.

In recent times very important work has been done in training parish leadership groups with a view to Parish Pastoral Councils. In the past Parish Councils concerned themselves mostly with bricks and mortar and the task of maintaining existing structures. The renewal format of Parish Pastoral Councils aims to have priests and people working together on all aspects of parish life with more emphasis on prayer, spirituality and faith formation rather than bricks and mortar. The working together of priests and people is essential if our Church is to be relevant in the new millennium. [102]

SUMMARY AND CONCLUSIONS

THE STATEMENT IN MATTHEW'S GOSPEL is a mission statement which is repeated in a different way in the other gospels and in Acts. The message is as clear today in the post-Vatican II eras as it was in the early church.

In this essay I examined the response to the statement in the early church. I outlined that difficult period in history for Christians up to AD 311. I examined the interpretations of the mission statement in documents from Vatican II and subsequent documents from the Holy See up to the present time. Since the bishops are the successors to the apostles, I studied their recent view from the USA Bishop's Conference in 2005. I researched the location and type of activity being carried out by Irish missionaries abroad and included practical examples of their great work in spite of the difficulties including martyrdom. Since any future effort in carrying out this mission statement is dependent on our youth today, I examined a sample of their views on religion and other matters. I also looked at some key points on ways to improve our understanding of youth today, with a view to involving them more in the life of the Church in the future

Finally, I have attempted to show how the Church is imitating the early church; giving examples of new activities and movements. I have involved the subject areas of Scripture, Church History and Spirituality (especially missionary spirituality) in my essay.

Challenges and Opportunities for the future

Our youth will take up the challenges of the future with the right leadership and encouragement and help especially from the Holy Spirit. The opportunities were never better in areas such as improved technology and transport. The hunger for education amongst the poor of the third world is also growing at an enormous rate. This is the fertile soil, the plough and the seed necessary to bring about basic change and subsequently the knowledge that Jesus exists and loves them.

Conclusions

I have drawn some conclusions from this study of the early church and the post-Vatican II church on 'Go Teach All Nations'. The major one is the increased admiration I have for the people in the early church and also for the priests and the religious in our Church today. The valuable contribution they have made is tremendous and should be supported generously by all.

The messenger has not changed. The message has not changed. Human nature has not changed. Communications and resources have improved enormously.

All of the above should have led to the result that the number of people knowing about Jesus is increasing all the time. In fact the opposite is the case. The number of people that haven't heard of Jesus is rising.

Jesus' command wasn't just intended for the disciples and missionaries. It was intended for us too. What we have to do—all we have to do—is to try to make sure our way of living and relating to others is Jesus' way. It is a difficult assignment but we can do it.

Bibliography

Africa, *St. Patrick's Missions*, October 2005.

Bishops Conference U.S.A., *Teaching the Spirit of Mission Ad Gentes Continuing Pentecost Today*, 2005.

Boran, George CSS P., *The Pastoral Challenges of a New Age*, Dublin: Veritas Publications, 1999.

Brown, Raymond, Joseph Fitzmyer and Roland Murphy. *The New Jerome Biblical Commentary*. New Jersey: Prentice Hall, 1999.

Brown R. E., *Introduction to the New Testament*, New York: Doubleday, 1999.

Christian Community Bible, Catholic Pastoral Edition. Manila: Divine Word Publications, 1991.

Drane, John. *Introduction to the New Testament*. Oxford: Lion Hudson PLC, 1999.

Dunne, Rev. T. *Lecture notes (the marriage feast of Cana)*. 13/09/05

Flannery, Austin O.P. *Vatican Council II*. New York: Costello Publishing Co., 1996.

Harvest Magazine, Winter 2005.

Irish Missionary Union, *Survey of Irish Personnel Overseas*. Dublin: Mount Argus, 2004.

Kerris, Robert. *The Collegeville Bible Commentary*. Minnesota: Liturgical Press, 1992,

Nenagh Community Network and Foroige, *Extract from Nenagh Youth Needs Analysis*, 2004.

Nenagh Parish Newsletter, 25/12/2005, 22/1/2006.

O'Dwyer, Rev. C., *Lecture Notes*, January 2004.

O'Neill, Stephen, *A History of Christian Missions*. United Kingdom: Penguin, 1990.

Pope John Paul II, *Address to Congregation for the Evangelization of Peoples*, 20/01/2001.
Pope John Paul II, *Redemptoris Mission*, 1990.
The Word Magazine, Dec.2005.
Vatican Council II, *Decree on The Ministry and Life of Priests, Presbyterorum Ordininis*, Ad Gentes 39, 1965.
Waters, E., CSSP, *Go Teach All Nations (A history of the Province of the Congregation of the Holy Spirit)*. Dublin: Paraclete press, 2000.

Endnotes

1. Raymond Brown et al, *The New Jerome Biblical Commentary* (New Jersey: Prentice Hall, 1999), 674

2. *Christian Community Bible*, Catholic Pastoral Edition (Manila: Divine Word Publications, 1991), 68.

3. *Christian Community Bible*, Catholic Pastoral Edition (Manila: Divine Word Publications, 1991), 68.

4. Ibid. 7.

5. Raymond Brown et al, *The New Jerome Biblical Commentary* (New Jersey: Prentice Hall, 1999), 674.

6. Ibid, P. 674

7. Ibid, P. 674

8. Robert Kerris, *The Collegeville Bible Commentary* (Minnesota: Liturgical Press 1992), 902.

9. John Drane, *Introduction to the New Testament*, (Oxford: Lion Hudson PLC, 1999) 104.

10. *Christian Community Bible*, Catholic Pastoral Edition (Manila: Divine Word Publications, 1991), 112.

11. Robert Kerris, *The Collegeville Bible Commentary*

(Minnesota: Liturgical Press 1992), 935.

12. Ibid. 979.

13. Raymond Brown et al, *The New Jerome Biblical Commentary* (New Jersey: Prentice Hall, 1999), 721.

14. Robert Kerris, *The Collegeville Bible Commentary* (Minnesota: Liturgical Press 1992), 1016.

15. Raymond Brown et al, *The New Jerome Biblical Commentary* (New Jersey: Prentice Hall, 1999), 974.

16. Robert Kerris, *The Collegeville Bible Commentary* (Minnesota: Liturgical Press 1992), 1004.

17. John Drane, *Introduction to the New Testament*, (Oxford: Lion Hudson PLC, 1999), 213.

18. *Christian Community Bible*, Catholic Pastoral Edition (Manila: Divine Word Publications, 1991), 232.

19. Ibid, 232.

20. Robert Kerris, *The Collegeville Bible Commentary* (Minnesota: Liturgical Press 1992), 1038.

21. John Drane, *Introduction to the New Testament*, (Oxford: Lion Hudson PLC, 1999), 264.

22. Pope John Paul II, *Redemptoris Missio*, (1990), 23.

23. Rev. C. O'Dwyer, *Lecture Notes*, Jan 2004.

24. Rev. C. O'Dwyer, *Lecture Notes*, Jan 2004.

25. Stephen O'Neill, *A History of Christian Missions*, (United Kingdom: Penguin, 1990), 8.

26. Rev. C. O'Dwyer, *Lecture Notes*, Jan 2004.

27. *Christian Community Bible*, Catholic Pastoral Edition (Manila: Divine Word Publications, 1991), 231.

28. Dunne, Rev. T., Lecture Notes, (13/09/05), P. 2

29. Rev. T. Dunne, *Lecture Notes*, (13/09/05), 5.

30. Ibid.

31. Stephen O'Neill, *A History of Christian Missions*, (United Kingdom: Penguin, 1990), 25.

32. John Drane, *Introduction to the New Testament*, (Oxford: Lion Hudson PLC, 1999), 274.

33. Ibid. 283.

34. R.E. Brown, *Introduction to the New Testament*, (New York: Doubleday, 1999), 298.

35. Rev. T. Dunne, *Lecture Notes*, (13/09/05), 5.

36. John Drane, *Introduction to the New Testament*, (Oxford: Lion Hudson PLC, 1999), 295.

37. Ibid. 317.

38. Austin Flannery, *O.P. Vatican Council II*, (New York: Costello Publishing Co., 1996), 444.

39. Pope John Paul II, *Redemptoris Missio Introduction*, (1990), 1–2.

40. Pope John Paul II, *Redemptoris Missio*, (1990), 19.

41. Ibid. 20.

42. Ibid. 21.

43. Ibid. 22.

44. Ibid. 26.

45. Ibid. 29.

46. Ibid. 31.

47. Ibid. 37.

48. Ibid. 39.

49. Ibid. 41.

50. Ibid. 44.

51. Ibid. 50.

52. Ibid. 50.

53. Ibid. 51.

54. Ibid. 52.

55. Ibid. 52.

56. Ibid. 55.

57. Ibid. 58.

58. Ibid. 59

59. Ibid. 65.

60. Vatican Council II, *Decree on The Ministry and Life of Priests, Presbyterorum Ordininis*, (1965), Ad Gentes 39.

61. Pope John Paul II, *Redemptoris Missio*, (1990), 69.

62. Ibid. 71.

63. Ibid. 72.

64. Ibid. 75.

65. Ibid. 75.

66. Ibid. 83.

67. Ibid. 88.

68. Ibid. 89.

69. Ibid. 90.

70. Ibid. 91.

71. Pope John Paul II, *Address to Congregation for the Evangelization of Peoples*, (20/01/2001), 1.

72. Bishops Conference U.S.A., *Teaching the Spirit of Mission Ad Gentes Continuing Pentecost Today*, (2005), 2.

73. Ibid.

74. Ibid. 3.

75. Ibid. 3.

76. Ibid. 4.

77. Ibid. 4.

78. Ibid. 5.

79. Ibid. 5.

80. Ibid. 5.

81. Ibid. 6.

82. Ibid. 6.

83. Irish Missionary Union, *Survey of Irish Personnel Overseas*, (Dublin: Mount Argus, 2004), 3.

84. Ibid. 21.

85. Ibid 22–42.

86. E Waters CSSP, *Go Teach All Nations*, (Dublin: Paraclete Press, 2000), 222.

87. Ibid. 323.

88. Ibid. 224–225.

89. Ibid. 225.

90. Irish Missionary Union, *Survey of Irish Personnel Overseas*, (Dublin: Mount Argus, 2004), 13.

91. *The Word Magazine*, (Dec.2005), 27.

92. Africa, *St Patrick's Missions*, (October 2005), 6–7.

93. *Nenagh Parish Newsletter*, (25/12/2005), 2.

94. *The Word Magazine*, (Dec.2005), 26.

95. Ibid. 26.

96. Ibid. 26–27.

97. George Boran CSSP, *The Pastoral Challenges of a New Age*, (Dublin: Veritas Publications, 1999), 11.

98. *Harvest magazine*, (Winter 2005), 13.

99. Nenagh Community Network and Foroige, *Extract from Nenagh Youth Needs Analysis*, (2004).

100. George Boran CSSP, *The Pastoral Challenges of a New Age*, (Dublin: Veritas Publications, 1999), 18.

101. Ibid. 118.

102. Bishop Willie Walsh, *Note in Nenagh Parish Newsletter*, (22/1/2006), 2.

V

THE WAY OF THE WISE IN THE BOOK OF PROVERBS

THE WAY OF THE WISE IN THE BOOK OF PROVERBS

TODAY THERE IS A MAJOR PROBLEM WITH PEOPLE, even well educated people, not saying what they believe or feel. We are all part of this Culture of speaking and writing. We tend to say what will be acceptable and then include a little of what we feel. Our writing is even more vague and full of hidden meanings. Most of the proverbs at least did pass on the words of wisdom as they were passed on to themselves and exactly how they felt about life. Otherwise there would have been total confusion about the words of wisdom. However, in some of the parables personification is used but there was a more valid reason for this than exists today.

> The Book of Proverbs is no less the word of God than the prophetic books : it is a different type of word, throwing a different light on Life. It does not deal with the destiny of God's people but with the possible ways for human beings to excel in every sense of the word. [1]

This statement helped to convince me that this subject would be a valuable experience. Also an extract from a Nigerean writer Bucha Emacheta helped: "Unwritten stories, prayers, lullabies, proverbs, riddles and songs, often told by older women were the means of passing on the wisdom and traditions of the Igbo people."[2]

I like the book of proverbs because the raw material is the human person in the real world with all its limitations. It appeals to what is most basic in human life. It teaches us how to live in the world no matter what out role is. Much of its teachings apply equally to pagans as well as to believers.

In this essay I will deal with the historical context of the wisdom literature and the place of the proverbs. I will discuss the literary form of the proverb and some of the factors which influenced it. I will also outline the structure of the Book of Proverbs and when the different sections were written. I will mention the use of personification as a method of teaching and the reasons for its use.

The proverbs seem to have sayings for every situation. I have chosen proverbs that are relevant to the family, the community, i.e. friends and neighbours, and others from society in general. In conclusion I will mention the relevance of the proverbs for me today and also mention some of he limitations people had at the time of writing the proverbs. I will conclude with an extract from the homily given by Pope John Paul at Limerick twenty-five years ago.

The historical context of wisdom literature and the social setting

Proverbs is the first in a group of five books generally regarded as the wisdom literature. This group includes Proverbs, Job, Ecclesiastes, Sirach and Wisdom.

The authors of these books were neither prophets or priests but scribes or "wise men." The main interest of the wise men was in the conduct of the individual human life.

They are distinguished from other biblical books by the following factors:

- Minimum interest in the great acts of salvation
- Little interest in Israel as a Nation or its history
- A questioning attitude to life and its problems
- A search for the ideal human life
- A great interest in the universal human experiences that effect all people
- Joy in the 'Contemplation of Creation and God as Creator.[3]

The setting in which wisdom literature was developed was most likely the Royal Court of David and Solomon. History has shown that the wise men of Egypt and Mesopotamia were considering the same problems as far back as 3000 years BC.

In the nomadic tribes of the desert the chief was the wise man. Wise sayings were handed down orally from one generation to the next. This literary form, which is called *Mashal* in Hebrew occupies the main part of the book of proverbs. Modern travellers in this geographical area come across these sayings even today. Writing gave a more permanent form to these sayings. The main purpose of proverbial wisdom was education. Many proverbs originated in the family long before the formation of the State of Israel. One can imagine the village elder advising young farmers-to-be "He who tills his own land has food in plenty, but he who follows idle pursuits is a fool" (Prov. 12:11). Solomon was the founder and patron of such a tradition. He was married to the daughter of an Egyptian Pharaoh, which must have helped to broaden his understanding. He also had the wealth to employ educated scribes to write down the proverbs. Some of the proverbs may have originated in the family and were subsequently edited by the tribe. Eventually they found their way into the Royal Court where they were written down. This idea is reinforced by the fact that many of the concerns as written were those of the middle class. Some of the teachings appear to be almost copied from an Egyptian wisdom writing known as the Teachings of Amenemope.[4]

The Literary form of the Proverbs

The literary form which is coded in Hebrew the *Mashal*, predominates in the Book of Proverbs, whose Hebrew title is *Mishle-Shelomah*—The Proverbs of Solomon:

> Writing made it possible to give a more permanent and developed form to the primitive Mashal, and the category was enlarged to embrace the fable, the parable, the allegory. [5]

The experience of exile was a major influence on the thinkers of Israel. It brought them into close contact with other cultures like Babylon, Egypt, Persia and gave them a universal view of Yahweh as not merely the God of Israel.

Almost all the wisdom literature is written in the style of

Hebrew poetry. It was not written in rhymes like our poetry but in parallel ideas called parallelism:

> It is constructed of two lines with some pre-designed relationship between each line. The most common form is synonymous Parallelism in which the second line repeats the idea of the first line, but uses different words e.g. Prov 4:1 "Listen children to the following construction and be attentive that you may gain insight. There is also parallelism i.e. of contrasting ideas. [6] e.g. Prov 10:1 "A wise child makes a glad father but a foolish child is a mother's heartbreak."
> The content of wisdom writing is important and profound, but the literary form represents a special Love for God that works potently with words and ideas until the most beautiful and effective way of expressing the content is achieved. The wisdom writers worshipped God with their minds. [7]

There are a lot of words that occur often in proverbs but rarely outside the wisdom books. Positive ones like wisdom, discipline, understanding, capacity, counsel, prudence and intelligence. Negative ones like simple, fool, stupid, scoffer, arrogant, Godless, lazy and impious. [8]

The Structure of the Proverbs

The sections that go back to Solomon could come from the period 960–920 BC i.e. 10:1—22:16. Proverb 25:1 describes one collection being made by King Hezekiah. This part of the book could possibly come from around 700 BC. We have no idea who King Lemuel and Agur were.The first section Chapters (1–9) is more recent. Most scholars agree that this section was part edited from the 5th to the 3rd century BC and some as late as the second century BC. From the beginning people are divided into two groups. The wise and the intelligent, clever and responsible and on the other hand the foolish, including all those who are stupid, lying and evil.

Chapters 1 to 9 are about excellence and the advantages of wisdom. Fear of the Lord is a good start. It recommends us to seek after wisdom as the best way of avoiding temptation more precious than all the Riches. Proverb 3:15 recommends men to practice virtue and avoid the wicked. Chapter 8 deals with the personal work of God. This could be a foreshadowing of the second person in the Trinity. Chapter 10 to 29 include 500 sayings and axioms related to wisdom and folly, virtue and vice.

Chapter 30 includes sayings of Agur Son of Jakeh. Chapter 31 includes the sayings of Lemuel and a poem in praise of the wise housewife.

The use of Personification in Proverbs

> The author of the prologue personifies wisdom as a Lady who goes about the street offering her precious gifts to men, inviting them to receive her confidences and to partake of her banquet table. In return for their acceptance she promises them true life and happiness. [9]

By using this means of communication he was able to overcome the problem of teaching the traditional religion of Israel to the ordinary people after they came out of exile from Babylon. The people were mainly poor, helpless peasants. Poverty and immorality were common. Theft, murder and adultery were the common crimes. There was anti-clerical feeling against restoring the cult of Yahweh. The use of personification seems to have worked under the guidance of divine inspiration.

The importance of God in the proverbs

> The spirit of the book of proverbs is essentially religious and the idea of God permeates the entire book. The introduction proclaims that 'Fear of he Lord is the beginning of wisdom' Prov. 3:15. It urges us to practise virtue, to flee the company of the wicked and to avoid the occasions of sin. [10]

Fear here means to have love and respect i.e. the person who fears Yahweh always takes him into account and bases his actions on God's word. Chapter 8 concentrates on the eternal word of God: "Yahweh created me first, at the beginning of his works. He formed me from of old, from eternity, even before the earth." Prov. 8:22–23.

Proverbs dealing with the Family

It is not surprising that the family is the basic concern in the proverbs, since many of the proverbs originated in the context of advise from one generation to the next e.g. Prov. 4:1,3–4, 10, 20. A stable sexual relationship between husband and wife is seen as the key to family stability. Adultery is singled out as a particularly destructive evil whose repercussions affect more than the two individuals involved.[11]

> The lips of another man's wife may be as sweet as honey and her kisses as smooth as olive oil, but when it is all over, she

> leaves you nothing but bitterness and poverty—Prov. 5:3–4.

The responsibility for bringing up children should be shared as indicated in Prov. 1:8–9, 6:20–21. There are also numerous references to instruction to children.

> Train children in the right way and when they are old, they will not stray—Prov. 22:6.
> Those who never chastise their children do them no favours but those who love them will be diligent to discipline them—Prov. 13:29

Proverbs dealing with friends and neighbours

> A neighbour near can help you more than a family member who is far away—Prov. 27:10
> Never tell your neighbour to wait until tomorrow if you can help them now—Prov. 3:28
> Don't visit your neighbour too often, they may get tired of you and come to hate you—Prov. 25:17

Gossip in these times, as in our time, was a big threat to friendship. This is covered in Prov. 18:8, 26:22.

Proverbs dealing with Society in general

> Better to be poor and fear the Lord than to be rich and in trouble. Better to eat vegetables with people you love than to eat the finest meat where there is hate—Prov. 15:16–17
> Better to be poor and honest than rich and dishonest—Prov 28:6.

At the beginning of the Book of Proverbs (Prov. 1:3) we hear the advice "To aquire well ordered knowledge, and become just with disernment and integrity." The Proverbs are full of advice to those who are rich to share what they have with the poor (Prov. 13:23 and 14:21, 31):

> Animals should be treated with due concern—Prov 14:4
> Speak up for people who cannot speak for themselves, protect the rights of all who are helpless, speak for them and be a righteous guide, protect the rights of the poor and needy—Prov 31:8–9.

Conclusion

In this essay I have attempted to set out the principal messages that I considered important. This covered the history, literary form, structure and the use of personification and the importance of God. I also sought out the proverbs that I thought were relevant to the family, the neighbours and society in general. There are some limitations in the proverbs. The most obvious limitation is that the wise men of that time did not know about the afterlife. They felt that wisdom and good living would be fully rewarded in this life. However, this has increased my personal admiration for them.

The second deficiency is the wise men's proposal that personal success is the key motive for the practice of justice. The New Testament resolved this by offering another reason in the Kingdom of God as established by Jesus Christ. The third deficiency is the treatment of women as second-class citizens. This was the culture of the time.

What message did I get from reading the proverbs for the first time?

Since they are the word of God they will always have an important value. They are the words of wisdom collected by an ancient people as a result of their experiences, which were different from my own. We cannot demand from them the insights which came with the teachings of Jesus. The proverbs show the qualities suitable for sensible living, being prudent and just and willing to forgive, being in control of my tongue and able to correct my children. In Israel of that time men would engage in talk at the gates as the women would look after the house and the children. The last poem urges all husbands to praise their wives and to be grateful to them.

In conclusion I am reminded of Pope John Paul's message at Limerick 25 years ago telling of the pressures on the family which are the same today even though more sophisticated. The people of the Old Testament had the same pressures:

> The Irish people have to choose today, their way forward. Will it be the substitution of a new ethic of temporal enjoyment for the law of God? [12]

Endnotes

1. *Christian Community Bible*, Catholic Pastoral Edition. (Manila: Divine Word Publications, 1991), 792.

2. H. Fallon, *Africa*, (Nov. 2004), 18.

3. Sr. M.T O'Brien, *Lecture Notes*, Sept.2004.

4. Hahn Roger, *Introduction to the Book of Proverbs*. (2003), 6.

5. J.T. Forristall, *CSB Proverbs*(1960), 6.

6. J. Drane, *Introduction to the Old Testament*, (Oxford:Lion Hudson PLC, 1999) 114.

7. Roger Hahn, *Introduction to the Book of Proverbs*. (2003), 5.

8. Summary Bergant D, *The Collegeville Bible Commentary—Old Testament*. (Minnesota: Liturgical Press,1992), 647.

9. J.T. Forristall, *CSB Proverbs*(1960) 8–9.

10. Sr. M.T O'Brien, *Lecture Notes*, Sept.2004.

11. J. Drane, *Introduction to the Old Testament*, (Oxford:Lion Hudson PLC, 1999) 114.

12. L. Power, *Word magazine* Nov. 2004, 5. Citing Pope John Paul's address in Limerick, 1979.

VI

SIGNIFICANT POINTS ABOUT ISLAM

SIGNIFICANT POINTS ABOUT ISLAM

I HAVE A NUMBER OF REASONS FOR choosing this topic. Firstly, Muslims are regularly in the news, for example in Iraq, Iran, Palestine, France and the United Kingdom. Muslims continue to claim that their religion is misunderstood and I don't want to be accused of this. Apart from attending lectures on world religions I wish to retain some basic facts on at least four world religions including Islam in order to be able to hold a sensible conversation on them without notes.

I am very interested in promoting peace and reconciliation and I feel that dialogue between religions will be very important in this regard.

The early history of Islam and the Qur'an .

Islam means Submission (i.e. to God) and also means Peace. There are opproximately 1.5 billion Muslims in the world and over 8 million in the USA alone. Like Judaism and Christianity, Islam arose in the Middle East. Mohammad was the founder in seventh century Arabia. Muslims believe it to be the faith actually practiced by Abraham, Moses, Noah and Jesus.The central document of muslims is the Qur'an or "Recitation" which is regarded by muslims as authorative and divine in nature. It offers a system for faithful living and guidance on all spheres of human behaviour. Although there are major differences in worldview among Chrisians,Jews and Muslims, the fundamental revelation of Mohammad i.e. One God does not conflict with core Christian or Jewish principles. It states there is one God,a God who requires of human beings both moral behaviour (action not simply belief) and pious devotion.

Islam teaches social and personal codes of conduct affecting both men and women. This is done in keeping with the dictates of the Sharia'ah, or law, which is rooted in the Qur'an and in the Sunnah.[1] Islamic culture has produced literary, scholarly and scientific works of note e.g. algebra.etc. Although Muslims deny the divinity of Jesus they honour him as a major prophet.

There are Five Pillars or major articles of faith in Islam:

- Belief in a single God called Allah.
- Belief in angels.
- Belief in revealed books.
- Belief in the Prophets.
- Belief in a day of judgement.

Mohammad was born around AD 570 in Mecca, a site of the ancient shrine known as the Ka'ba, which is traditionally associated with Abraham. His father was a merchant. He is regarded by muslims as the final prophet of God, the last in a long series of prophets which includes Moses and Jesus. His father and mother died shortly after his birth and he was reared by relations. At the age of twenty-four, Mohammad married a wealthy widow and became a prosperous merchant in his community. At the age of forty he believed he was summoned by God to proclaim the word of the supreme and single God Allah. He attracted followers but earned the ridicule of the chiefs.

As Mecca was already a pilgrim city for many gods they were afraid of losing their status as a place of pilgrimage. Mohammad's family also fell out with him and his life was threatened. In 622 he organised an exodus (Hegirain) of his followers to Medina. That journey to Medina,a place then known as Yathrib,was as essential to the Islamic faith as was Exodus for the Jewish people. [2] That year is celebrated as the first year of the muslim era. He attracted many followers in Medina and engaged in a military conflict with Mecca which he captured. Islam was now a state religion in Mecca and more consolidated. In 632 Mohammad died in Medina.

The Qur'an

Given to Mohammad in a cave by the angel Gabriel in AD 632, this is the scripture for Muslims as the Gospels are for Christians and the Torah for Jews. It also has parallels in the wisdom literature of the Bible. Muslims evolved and created a theme or belief akin or parallel to the description of God found in the Torah and in Wisdom Literature–Proverbs 8:22–26;8:27–30;8:35–36. That theme included the belief that God's wisdom had been present from the origin of the Universe.[3] The essential theme in the Qur'an is God is the creator,controller and final judge of everything. It accepts Christians and Jews as people of the book. It was written between 610 and 632. It has 114 Surahs or chapters. A few of the most important ones are 1, 112, 113, and 114 which deal with openness, surety of unity and refuge. The Qur'an is not sequential (i.e.from Adam to Mohammad) but focuses on themes such as:

- Relationship with God
- God's unique attributes
- Human accountability
- Day of judgement
- Ethics
- Social justice
- Rise and fall of nations
- The natural world and family issues.

Allah as the creator of man is contained in Surah 16:3 and many rules for morals are contained in Surahs 10:89–97. Rules for kindness to parents can be found in 46:15–19 and the concepts of humility,self-respect, veneration of God, tolerance and Laity are mentioned in Surahs 25:65–76.

Muslims believe that they are decended from Ishmael who was the first son of Abraham by his servant Hagar and later exiled.

The Five Pillars

The Qur'an outlines five pillars or obligations essential to the lives of Muslims:

- Declaration of faith in God

- Prayer five times daily
- Zaket or alms to the poor : at least 2.5% of disposable income
- Fasting e.g. Ramadan etc.
- At least one pilgrimage (Hajj) to Mecca in a lifetime

The main groups within Islam

Today 85% of Muslims are Sunni or orthodox with emphasis on fundamentals but culturally and religiously diverse. They have opted for a broadly accepted set of theological principles. Sunnis do not have a structured religious hierarchy.

The Shias place heavy emphasis on the role of individual clerics. The word Shia means follower. They originated after a bitter seventh century dispute over succession to Islamic leadership after the death of Mohammad and his son in law Ali. Early on the Shias emerged in opposition to the central government and supported the claim that the leadership must be decended from Mohammad through his son in law Ali. There is a direct line of decendants up to Mohammad Al-Muntazar who disappeared in AD 878 and who is still considered the only ligimate leader today. Shia clerics today are considered deputies of the twelve Imams and are called Mullahs or Mujtahids. Shia Islam is the official religion of Iran,and worshippers in India, Pakistan, Iraq, and other areas. They make up about 15% of the world population of Muslims.

Most Shias belong to a group known as imamites or the twelve imam division. A smaller sect is that of the Ismailites,who acknowledge seven Imams.

The Sufis are another goup. They are the mystics of islam.

Every faith has mystics i.e. men and women who seek union with God through contemplation, asceticism and prayer. They engage in fasting, going without sleep, tolerating rough conditions etc. They both enrich and threaten their religious establishment.

The daily life of Muslims, their places of worship, and holy days etc.

Sunni muslims have five main prayers, each connected to a particular time of the day i.e. five times. Shias pray three times daily. The prayers can be said in the Mosque or other suitable places. The Mosque is a place of prayer with a central point that orients worship towards Mecca. Friday is the Islamic Sabbath day. Attendance for males is compulsory. Men and women pray separately. Muslim prayers make use of memorized recitations. A non-practicing muslim is not allowed to join the prayer line

There is also a separate place in the mosque for non-muslims. For reasons of modesty, girls and women cover thrir heads and necks, although there are no hard and fast rules. Muslims have their own ceremonies for initiation (Shahada generally at mid teens), marriage, funerals etc. They must be buried within 24 hours of death. Holy days, e.g.Ramadan, last for a whole month. Between sunrise and sunset they abstain from eating, drinking, smoking, sex etc. This feast is movable depending on a lunar calendar. Islam has other holy days also based on the lunar calendar.

The belief of Muslims in the Afterlife.

To devout muslims the events of this life are seen as a trial from Allah for the life to come. They believe in a day of judgement, when Allah will raise all humanity and each will account for his/her own actions, with the consequences of hell or heaven. Ultimately they believe that it is Allah who will determine the fate of each human being. Several passages of the Qur'an suggest that devout Christians and Jews can attain paradise. The antichrist will appear on the day of judgement and will be defeated by Jesus who will affirm the faith of Islam. Muslims believe that angels are important in life as well as at the time of death.

Muslims today, their ethnic origin, the role of women, the meaning of Jihad, suicide and the seventy-two virgins

Islam is the least understood of the three monontheistic faiths. Today most muslims are non-arab. To treat all muslims as though they came from the middle east would be to ignore the diversity and the historical influences of the Islamic faith. There is a common belief that islam oppresses women. The vast majority of muslim women reject this notion. The oft-quoted phrase "Slay the unbelievers" in the Qur'an refers to a time when the muslim world was at war.

The seventy-two virgins are not mentioned in the Qur'an and in fact it forbids suicide in all situations. This legend is dubiously attributed to Mohammad, a saying that has nothing whatever to do with suicide attacks. Jihad should not be translated as holy war. The word means effort, especially against one's own imperfections. Only in extreme cases is there a duty to fight against unbelieving enemies.

Conclusion

Having examined a number of references on islam I have learned many points which I have found interesting for the following reasons:

- The history of islam and its relationship to Christianity.
- The different groups within Islam and why some are so opposed to others
- The daily prayers and place of worship of Islam
- The importance of the Qur'an and how it can be misinterpreted just as the bible has been misinterpreted.

Also, on the role of women there is an urgent need for a survey to clarify the position for the western world. There is also a need for polititians and journalists and scholars to clarify many of the prevailing misconceptions that exist today. I also found the muslim view of the afterlife interesting.

In conclusion I am pleased that I chose this topic. I feel that I have learned a great deal more about Islam which will help me to reduce barriers in the future. Some scholars of Islam feel that the Qur'an could be adapted, so that it would be less uncompromising. However the vision of Jesus was focused on love rather than law. This is seen in the Sermon on the Mount,where one is encouraged to love one's enemies.Hence, perhaps an ethical or theological humanitarianism could be stressed over the law.[4]

Endnotes

1. T. Toropov and Rev. L. Buckles, *World Religions 3rd Edition*, (Indianapolis : Alpha Books, 2004), 122.

2. Russel Marie Cummins, *Lecture Notes,* 6/12//2005.

3. Ibid.

4. Ibid.

VII

THE PHENOMENON OF ATHEISM

THE PHENOMENON OF ATHEISM

THERE ARE A NUMBER OF REASONS FOR THE subject matter of this essay. I need to be able to discuss the subject of Atheism generally. I also need extra information on Philosophy, Psychology and Sociology in order to take part in a fruitful conversation on the influence of these subjects on Atheism. Having studied most of the physical and biological sciences, I also need to enhance my views on Atheism and the influence science has had on the subject up to the present.

In writing this essay I will be able to familiarize myself with the names of people who made important contributions to these subjects.

In a few years time I hope to study the subjects of philosophy and psychology in more detail. In the meantime, I will be satisfied if I can hold a reasonable conversation on these subjects.

Indifference leading to a form of atheism based on agnosticism is the biggest challenge of today. The positive end of this fact is that many of the people who feel this way are educated and intelligent. They will engage in an intelligent discussion and are very receptive to facts based on evidence and are not as dismissive as we may suspect. A profound knowledge of each subject is not necessary for such a discussion. However, a knowledge, based on some study and research is extremely valuable. These are some of the principle reasons I have chosen to write this topic on the contribution of all these subjects to the phenomenon of Atheism.

In this article, I will look at the definition of Atheism and some of the types of Atheism. I will also discuss some of the history of Atheism, though not in great detail. I will write about the contribution of philosophy and the themes of the people involved. I will discuss psychology, with special reference to Sigmund Freud and his contribution to the phenomenon of Atheism. I am including Sociology with other sciences in their contribution to Atheism. My reason for this is that the over-dependence on science by society to solve its problems seems to coincide with the study of sociology as a serious scientific study in the 19th Century.

What is Atheism

Atheism in everyday usage, means the denying of the existence of God and in practice living as if God did not exist.

> The existence of God is seen as an obstacle to the affirmation of the autonomy of man. Atheism can be theoretical, that is, denying at an intellectual and explicit level that God exists and practical, that is, living as if God does not exist,

without showing much concern about whether God exists or not at a theoretical level. This type of atheism is more dangerous, because it manifests an attitude of indifference toward God and religion. [1]

History of Atheism

Socrates was accused of being *atheos,* although he is said to have claimed inspiration from a divine voice. This atheism was often used to describe something like heresy or impiety. One of the oldest known atheists was Epicurus around 200 BC. The main aim of his followers was to attain peace of mind by exposing fear of divine wrath as irrational. The movement was marginal and gradually died out at the end of the Roman Empire, until it was revived by Pierre Gassendi, in the 17th Century. The term atheist was coined in the 16th Century and mutually used against people who represented a threat to established beliefs.

After the French revolution of 1789, Atheism received political notability and opened the way for the 19th Century movements of free thought and liberalism.

The transformation can be described as a change from a classical view of the world which was static i.e. unchangeable and reflecting the will of God. The new historical view was influenced by the expressions *liberty, equality, fraternity*. Reason was pitted against religion, science against dogma, tolerance against oppression. In many countries, denying God was included under the definition of the crime of Blasphemy. In Germany, Spain and the United Kingdom, these laws remain on the statute books, as in some American states, but they are rarely enforced if at all.

State support of atheism and oppression to organized religion has been the policy of most communist countries, including China, and the Former Soviet Union. Some churches were tolerated, but were subject to strict control. Consequently the Catholic Church was amongst the staunchest opponents of communist regimes: "Atheism has philosophical, psychological, sociological and empirical roots." [2]

Philosophical Contributions to Atheism

The question that arises here is, "How can we affirm God as the Creator, author of life, God of history etc. and at the same time affirm man as a unique individual, an irreducible being, source, meaning and an end in and to himself? God and man cannot both survive. One must die, let it be God." [3] The development of modern science alienated some people from the world of the sacred and the focus began to shift from God to man and from religion to science. Rene Descartes (1596–1650) contributed most to this shift with his formulation *Cogito ergo sum*—I think therefore I exist. Man becomes the centre of his own thinking, meaning and value:

> At first sight it may strike one as odd to see the thought of Descartes described as a significant source of atheism for the man himself was a convinced Christian...Descartes' philosophic revolution consisted in calling into question the reality of the external word and depicting man's quest for a basic framework of meaning, certitude and value, inwards to the resolve of his own subjectivity rather than outwards to a divinely formed external world immediately given in sensible living. [4]

Emmanuel Kant (1724–1804) further affirms the universal autonomy of man. Man, not God, is the foundation of truth and value. God exists to make moral discourse possible and be a rewarder. God is necessary to make sure morality makes sense:

> If we cannot validly speculate beyond experience to the existence of a supreme being as the ultimate ground of all things, then by the same token we cannot speculate beyond experience to the non existence of the Supreme being. [5]

George Hegel (1770–1831) believed that God is nothing but the full flowering of man. He compromises the absolute freedom of God in creation. He also compromises God in saying that God needs the world to fulfill himself.

Fuerbach (1804–1872)

Karl Barth remarks "Having proceeded far beyond Hegel as well as Kant, Fuerbach belongs to the Berlin master's disciples who scented the theological residue in his teaching and stripped it off .[6] For whereas religion embodies merely a pre reflective projection of human attributes as an illusory divine being, theology compounds this alienation by taking the transcendent divine subject as to whom the human attributes have been projected as the absolute and veridical starting point in its reflections."[7]

Ludvig Feurbach is the first explicit atheist. There is no theology for him only anthropology. All the Christian doctrines are not revealed, but have a human basis. God is only there because man has put him there. Man created God out of his own need to be great. There is only a God for me.

Karl Marx (1818–1883)

An atheist who wrote in his Critique of Hegel's *Philosophy of Right*:

> Religious suffering is at one and the same time, the expression of real suffering and a protest against real suffering. Religion is the sigh of the oppressed creature, the heart of a heartless world, and the soul of soulless conditions. It is the opium of the people. [8]

Marx argued that what is required in society is action, revolutionary action to eliminate the inhuman basis which gave rise to religious illusion. The radical and original source of unhappiness is the exploitation of man by man. He believed that religion was bad, which would be proved when communism arrived. Nietzsche (1844–1900) believed that the survivor is the fittest, man cannot affirm his own autonomy if he accepts God.

The Contribution of Psychology to Atheism

> Freud sees three levels in the human mind (psyche) namely, superego (Parental influence) ego, (conscious experience) and id (unconscious elements). Id contains the basic instincts of human nature. There is no sense of order or value there. Id contains such forces as Eros, Thatanos and repressed experiences. When we do not come to terms with these forces we remain neurotic.[9]

He believed religion is an expression of man's repressed feelings. He also felt that science would liberate us.

Freud's great contribution is the discovery of the Id. All the forces that affect us from within are not obvious. In a moment of weakness all the devils can come out. However, his conclusions are not really scientific but general projections. Religion can be alienating but can be creative too.

The central concept of Freud's work aside from the unconscious is the well known Oedipus Complex in which, the father lauded over all the women, the jealous sons kill the father and then felt guilty. In remorse they offer rituals to the father. The memory of the dead father eventually becomes God.

Professor Paul C. Vitz of New York University carried out a study of the fathers of some prominent atheists e.g. Freud, Marks, Fuerbach, O'Hair, Holbach, Russel, Nietzsche, Sartre, and Camus. He took biographical information from standard references sources. He found a defective case relationship with the father in each case, and is developing a defective father hypothesis. He says, "More evidence needs to be obtained. But the information already available is substantial; it is unlikely to be an accident." [10]

However, we should not lose sight of the combined influence of eminent psychologists, because they highlight a fact very few of us want to face i.e. that religion can be an escape from reality, and our responsibilities. Adherence to religious duties, rites and obligations often arises from fear of the consequences rather than from genuine personal conviction. It is the task of psychologists to examine our motives in openness and truth.

The contribution of Science to Atheism

The growth of positive science under Copernicus, Gallileo, Newton from the 15th Century to the 18th Century and the understanding of the physical universe was very important:

> It displaced the traditional, well defined notion of a hierarchical, finite cosmos which fostered such ready acceptance of Supra traditional, spiritual, and divine realities. [11]

On Comte and Spencer, Diarmuid O'Murchu comments as follows:

> Both consider religion to have been the mainstay of an earlier culture now displaced by an emerging secular civilization in which religion would become largely if not totally redundant...Comte envisaged a positivist society, governed by scientists and intellectuals working in close liaison with industrialists. This positivism would provide for society what Christianity had done for Europe right through the middle ages, creating intellectual certainty, moral consensus and social stability. [12]

Up to the time of the French Revolution, religion and the state were the unifying forces in society. After this period of turmoil religion became a private affair. Comte believed that the disappearance of traditional religion initiated a crisis in society. Sociology studies society in all its aspects. As a distinct subject it only dates to 1840s when given a chair at the University of Paris. In the beginning religion was regarded as superstitious nonsense. It adopted the empirical method of study. Sociology as a result tended towards determinism i.e. a denial of free will. It tended to exclude whatever could not be proven scientifically.

After the First World War had shown that more science produced more guns, religion kept coming back. Sociology adopted the rational or speculative method as well as the empirical, i.e. Ask first. What is the ideal? The resulting method of study was ideals, goals and the empirical method. Free will is a facility that must be used.

The Chinese government still considers science and belief to be opposites to each other. They publicly proclaim that scientific knowledge will break Theism. However, they cannot dispute the fact that countries that are more religious are more advanced in science and technology. Isaac Newton and Albert Einstein had a deep understanding of religion and God. In China the definition of "Freedom of religious belief" is not allowing the people to believe in any religion. There are statements such as:

> It is the responsibility of a modern country to educate and disseminate scientific Atheism to the public. But due to different reasons, many developed countries do not fulfill this responsibility. [13]

These sayings are able to deceive the Chinese people because their Government has isolated them from the rest of the world. China is very important in relation to atheism since it has a big portion of the world's population.

Conclusions

In this essay on the Contribution of Philosophy, Psychology and Science to the phenomenon of Atheism, I have attempted to set out the principal points I consider important. These covered the definition and the history of Atheism. I sought out the views of noted philosophers, a psychologist and other commentators on Science etc.

Many of us have been blessed with an upbringing in an environment that made belief in God much easier than for many others who have suffered more or have been raised in a spiritually impoverished environment or had other difficulties to cope with. Pope John Paul II was a philosopher and a great believer in the rights of people to choose which faith or no faith they choose to believe in with their own consciences. In this way he was able to open dialogue with many faiths that had previously felt they were being preached at. Scripture makes it clear we are not to judge others, however much we are called to correct evil.

To a person of deep faith no explanation of the existence of God is necessary. To a person who will not believe, no explanation is adequate. As the psalmist says "the man greedy for gain curses and renounces the Lord. In the pride of his countenance the wicked does not seek Him; all his thoughts are 'There is no God'" (psalm 10:3–4).

What message did I get from this topic?

At the end of the day my belief is based on the faith handed down from my parents and the Catholic Church. I am reminded of Pope John Paul's message at Limerick 25 years ago telling of the pressures on the family which are the same today even-though more sophisticated:

> The Irish people have to choose today their way forward. Will it be the substitution of a new ethic of temporal enjoyment for the Law of God. [14]

I hope I will be able to have a reasonable discussion on this subject in the future. A 2004 survey by the BBC in ten countries showed the proportion of "people who don't believe in God nor in a higher power" varying between 0 and 30% with an average close to 10% in the countries surveyed. About 8% of the respondents stated specifically that they consider themselves to be atheists.

Bibliography

Putti, Dr J. *Lecture Notes*, March 2005.

Masterson P, *Atheism and Alienation*, 1971.

Marx K, *Critique of Hegels Philosophy of the Right,* 1843.

Vltz, Prof Paul. C, *Psychology of Atheism*, Truth Journal New York University — http://www.leaderu.com/truth/itruth12.html, 2004.

O Murchu Diarmuid,*The God who became redundant*, 1986.

Folunfafa in Europe, Thoughts on Scientific Atheism — http://www.clearharmony.net/articles/2005.

Word magazine, November, 2004.

Lacroix Jean, *The Meaning of Atheism*, 1965.

Kaufman. G, *God the Problem*, 1972.

Endnotes

1. Dr. J. Putti, *Lecture Notes*, March 2005.
2. Ibid.
3. Ibid.
4. P. Masterson, *Atheism and Alienation* (1971), 9.
5. Ibid. 24.
6. P. Masterson, *Atheism and Alienation* (1971), 63.
7. Ibid. 69.
8. Karl Marx, *Critique of Hegels philosophy of the right.*
9. Dr. J. Putti, *Lecture Notes*, March 2005.
10. Prof Paul. C Vltz, *Psychology of Atheism.*
11. P. Masterson, *Atheism and Alienation*, (1971), 4.
12. Diarmuid O'Murchu, *The God who became redundant*, 94.
13. Thoughts on Scientific Atheism Clear harmony – Folun defa in Europe www.clearharmony . net/articles/2005
14. Word magazine,(Nov 2004) cited Pope John Paul 1979

VIII

MARRIAGE AT THE HEART OF GOD'S PLAN

MARRIAGE AT THE HEART OF GOD'S PLAN

I LOOKED FORWARD TO WRITING THIS ESSAY for a number of reasons. It gave me the opportunity to study marriage from a number of different perspectives while providing me with an opportunity to examine the present day attitude to marriage. In addition, I hope it will help me in my own marriage journey.

In this essay, I will deal with God's plan for marriage going back over three thousand years. I will discuss marriage in the Old Testament and the customs and practices of the time. I will mention what Jesus said about marriage as related in the New Testament. Vatican II spent a lot of time discussing marriage and *Humane Vitae* was introduced a few years later by Pope Paul VI. I will also be commenting on the family as a miniature church and the idea of marriage as a contract or a covenant and discussing the question of whether God's plan for marriage is being rejected today.

A stroke of luck is a little piece of fiction added to give the reader a lift. I will finish with two prayers for a couple getting married, one written over two thousand years ago and the other written recently.

What is Marriage?

Marriage is a concept as old as humanity. It is the way that society has devised to organize itself. No better way has been found that is accepted across cultures and generations. Despite many attacks, it is still presented as the ideal for most couples as well as for Christians:

> God's eternal plan is that all men and women should participate and share in the divine life and being. The Father summons people to realize this plan, in union with their fellow human beings, thus forming the people of God (cf. *Luman Gentium*, 9). In a special way the family is called to carry out this divine plan...God created us in his own image (Genesis 1;26) and gave us the mission to increase and multiply, to fill the earth and subdue it (Genesis 1;28). To carry out this plan man and woman are joined in an intimate union of love for the service of life. God calls spouses to participate in His creative power by handing on the gift of life. [1]

In the second story of creation we begin to see more on the place of marriage in God's plan; i.e. the Yahweh tradition, called so because the author, around 961–922 BC, called God Yahweh. This account links marriage and the family to the very heart of God's plan. Here God's intention is seen to create a companion for the man and have them live together in unity and intimacy (Genesis 2: 21–24). God intended marriage as a covenant of oneself in heart, mind and body. God created man and woman equal. Just as marriage is at the heart of God's plan unity and love are central to this divine plan.

Marriage in the Old Testament

God is the author of marriage, not some human arrangement devoid of God. Monogamy is the form of marriage presented in the norm even though other forms are present e.g. Divorce in the Old Testament was allowable. This was done mainly to regulate and protect women, since men could walk away from situations. Women had little rights though they had a high status due to child-bearing. Marriage was entered into by arrangement of families. Dates were set. The man simply took the woman into his home. Sometimes a marriage contract was drawn up beforehand e.g. (TOB, 7:1–20). [2]

By the time of Ezra towards the end of the Old Testament period it was assumed that one man would marry one woman, and both would be ethnically Israelite. In earlier times, though, it was the common practice for a man to have several wives, and not only was the practice never explicitly forbidden, but also almost all the leading male characters in the Old Testament stories had multiple regular sexual partners, who were not necessarily their wives, nor were they all Israelites. The list of Solomon's wives and partners reads like a roll call of all the nations of the ancient world. [3]

Marriage in the New Testament

The New Testament presents a new image of marriage. It is

used to illustrate the closeness of God to his Israel. Only a free people could marry. Slaves were allowed marry if the master permitted it. Children of slaves could not marry. Romans could not marry slaves. There wasn't any involvement of the authority in marriage. Consent was sufficient. The Church absorbed much of the Roman system. It rejected the option to exit marriage. There was no involvement of clergy at the beginning. Clandestine marriages were allowed i.e. no witnesses present. Later a priest and two witnesses were required. It is the same today.

Jesus spoke of the relationship of husband and wife when he declared to the Pharisees, "Haven't you read, that at the beginning the Creator made them male and female, and because of this, a man has to leave father and mother and be joined to his wife, and the two shall become one body. So they are no longer two, but one body? Therefore let no one separate what God has joined" (Mark 10: 5–9).

The Influence of Vatican 11

The equality of the sexes was stressed. Man and woman were both created from the same source. It saw marriage as a covenant of love not to be broken. This is the present understanding as noted in *Guadium et Spes,* Paragraph 48. Marriage is an intimate partnership or sharing of mutual life and love. It also added that marriage has been founded by the Creator and is governed by His laws, and that marriage is formed by the marital covenant whose nature is one of inescapable personal covenant. In summary, Paragraph 48 indicates God's authorship of marriage. Some of the canons associated with this document were not completed until 1977 which I will discuss later.

Humane Vitae was published by Pope Paul VI in 1968. This tells us that the conjugal act itself must be fully human, totally exclusive and open to new life. In short it banned contraception. This caused a major controversy in the Catholic Church which continues to this day. This is a very broad subject and deserves a separate essay, so I will not go into it for this essay.

The family as a Miniature Church

St John Chrysostum (347–407), Patriarch of Constantinople and doctor of the Church, described Christian marriage and the family as "A miniature Church" (Homily 20, on Ephesians 5: 22–33).

Like the Church at large, a marriage is a place where God reigns and where Jesus is present. It is a small version of the whole body of Church, a place where the members of the family, like the members of the Church, are united by the Holy Spirit. The parents have the principal responsibility to lead each other and their children to holiness and to acknowledge Jesus. The second Vatican council said something similar:

> The family is so to speak, the domestic Church. In it parents should, by their word and example, be the first preachers of faith to their children. [4]

Marriage a Contract or a Covenant

For several hundred years marriage had come to be regarded as a contract, sacred for Christians but no longer demanding love as an essential element. Love, permanence and exclusiveness are demanded but not the substance. The right of the body of the other person must be permanent and exclusive, but not the right to the person's love and affection:

> Contracts deal with things, covenants with people. Contracts engage the services of people, covenants engage persons. Contracts are made for a specific period of time, covenants are forever. Contracts can be broken, covenants cannot be broken. Contracts can be made by children who know the value of a penny; Covenants can be made only by adults who are mentally, emotionally and spiritually mature.[5]

The canons 242.1 and 242.2 were finalized in May 1977 to read:

> The marital covenant, by which a man and a woman create between themselves an intimate sharing in all life, a sharing of its nature oriented to the good of the spouses and to the procreation and nurture of children, has been raised, when it is of baptized persons, to the dignity of a sacrament— 242.1

> Marital consent is an act of the will by which a man and a woman give themselves and accept one another in an irrevocable covenant in order to create a marriage— 242.2

A married person might not use complex language like this! *Gaudium et Spes,* Chapter 1, paragraph 11 contains the master idea in a view of marriage which had been lost or obscured for centuries i.e. Marriage is likened to God's covenant with Israel and Christ's covenant with the Church.

Is Gods plan for marriage being rejected?

A single mother deserves all the help she gets and more. Despite all this, single mothers or single parents as a group are amongst the least well-off in our society. Surely God's plan for marriage is better if it is possible. Our present divorce law of No Fault Divorce means that a mother and child or father and child can be party to a divorce which is against their wishes. New EU regulations may further shorten the time needed to acquire a divorce.

In Co. Meath 40% of all children born at the present time are born outside of marriage. Someone should ask the children how they feel about this. We have no right to be critical or to show any lack of support for families in other situations. We should provide help and support to them in their difficult task of rearing children.

Same sex marriage

> Whether you believe in a creator God or a humanistic evolutionary model, the fact remains that human sexuality is best suited to occur between a man and a woman. To ignore this obvious fact is nonsensical. To sanction the opposite through same sex marriage is cultural suicide. [6]

Marriage Breakdown

> The Church is deeply saddened when some marriages, for various reasons, fail. The Church provides sensitive and compassionate pastoral care for people who find themselves in difficult marriages or family situations and is committed to encouraging their participation in the life and mission of Christ, through involvement in their own parishes. [7]

A Stroke of Luck

Before the stroke he was convinced that marriage was beneath him. But after being brought low, Joe saw that marriage is extraordinary. Two people throw the dice together or dive into deep water over and over again, terrified and thrilled that they cannot control the outcome. This is surely the greatest adventure of a lifetime for many, surely better than living together for ten years and having it all worked out.

Joe got down on one knee, "Molly, I ask you, will you marry me?"

Pause…Everything hangs in the balance…Still no answer.

"Are you joking"

"No I am not joking." Joe got up, looked at Molly, "I really want to marry you."

"Yes"

"Yes?"

"Yes!"

They jumped up and down hugging and kissing. They are in this together.

A Prayer for a couple getting married

The following prayer is over two thousand years old:

Happy the husband of a really good wife, the number of his days will be doubled. A perfect wife is a joy to a husband, he will live out the years of his life in peace. A Good wife is the best of portions reserved for those who fear the Lord. Rich or poor, they will be glad of heart, cheerful of face, whatever the season. [8]

A Modern Prayer

We pray for all married couples that they may empower each other to grow as persons and to grow in their love for each other.

Conclusion

In this essay I have set out my reasons for believing that marriage is at the heart of God's Plan. Marriage is seen as a good plan by most societies and religions in the world and the best way to organize itself and its society. I have examined marriage in the Old Testament from the book of Genesis up to the time of Jesus. In the New Testament I looked at the culture of the Romans and how the Church accepted much of that culture on marriage. In the New Testament I have mentioned the teaching of Jesus to the Pharisees as outlined in Marks Gospel. I used information from Vatican II on marriage and the arguments over marriage being a contract or a covenant which need the involvement of married people to help in producing more understandable wording.

I mentioned how God's plan for marriage is being rejected in today's world and some of the consequences. Finally I found two prayers for married couples, one from the Old Testament and the other from today.

What did I get from this essay?

I found this essay more difficult than I thought it would be initially. As a married person who has helped to rear a family with my wife and having made many mistakes, I feel that I am learning all the time, and that marriage is something to be worked at constantly throughout my life. This article has made me more aware of marriage as a sacrament and a covenant for life and that the Holy Spirit is always available to help in difficult times.

1. Bishops' Conference of Scotland, *Marriage and the Family*, (02/02/2004)

2. Rev. Fr. C Tierney, *Lecture Notes*, (Nov 2004).

3. John Drane, *Introducing the Old Testament*, (Oxford:Lion Publishing, 2000), 28.

4. Vatican Council II, *On The Church*.

5. Paul F. Palmer, *Needed: A Theology of Marriage*, International Catholic Review, Fall 2004. 253.

6. MD Staver, *Same sex marriage, putting every household at risk*, (2002), 100–102

7. Bishops' Conference of Scotland, *Marriage and the Family*, (02/02/2004).

8. Sirach (26: 1-4).